The Home Office Solution

The Home Office Solution

How to Balance Your Professional and Personal Lives While Working at Home

Alice Bredin
with Kirsten Lagatree

John Wiley & Sons, Inc.

New York · Chichester · Weinheim · Brisbane · Singapore · Toronto

This publication is designed to provide accurate and authoritative information in regard to the subject matter covered. It is sold with the understanding that the publisher is not engaged in rendering legal, accounting, or other professional services. If legal advice or other expert assistance is required, the services of a competent professional person should be sought.

Library of Congress Cataloging-in-Publication Data
Bredin, Alice.
    The home office solution: how to balance your professional and personal lives while working at home / Alice Bredin with Kirsten Lagatree.
      p. cm.
    Includes index.
    ISBN 0-471-19209-0 (alk. paper)
    1. Home-based businesses. 2. Quality of life. 3. Quality of work life.
    4. Telecommuting—Psychological aspects. I. Lagatree, Kirsten M. II. Title.
    HD62.38.B73   1998
    658'.041—dc21   97-31545

Printed in the United States of America
10 9 8 7 6 5 4 3 2 1

CONTENTS

Part Two Managing Time and Workload

Part Three Integrating Your Work Life and Private Life

Part Four Health

Acknowledgments

So many people helped me to create this book that I am truly thankful for the opportunity to put my appreciation in writing. Kirsten Lagatree is a talented researcher and writer who helped build the foundation for the book. She also has an extraordinary sense of humor and an enviable vocabulary that make any project we work on together a great learning experience for me as well as lots of fun. Stuart Feil is a keen editor and writer whose intelligence and insight continually impress me. He used his creativity and good judgment to shape and edit the book and it benefited greatly from his involvement.

Thanks go to my smart, energetic agent, Jane Dystel, for her encouragement and ongoing guidance and to Tom Miller, my editor at John Wiley & Sons, whose leadership guided me through the process of editing the book.

I also appreciate the assistance of the many telecommuters, home-based entrepreneurs, and other authorities who shared their knowledge with me for the book. Their time and effort made the book possible.

As with all of my work, my mother and sister deserve credit for enhancing this book with their creativity and their love and support of me. My husband and best friend, Stu, makes it all fun, possible, and worthwhile.

Introduction

Look in any apartment building, housing development, or neighborhood and you will find home offices. Approximately 30 million people worked in home offices in 1997, an 18 percent increase over 1995 numbers. This is only the beginning; the number of people working at home will continue to grow rapidly in the next few years and in the decades to come.

A home office refers to any space in the home devoted to conducting business or completing work for your employer. It can be a desk in the corner of a room, a space in the garage or basement, or even a room that is semiattached to your home. I have seen offices in the foyers of apartments, in the cupolas of Victorian houses, and in small, freestanding buildings in people's backyards. If someone works at home as a wage earner for an employer, he or she is a called a telecommuter. The other kind of home office worker is someone who runs a business at home. This person is called a home-based entrepreneur.

Several factors are driving the growth of the work-at-home population. Major employers have realized that allowing employees to work at home is a means of attracting and retaining good workers, increasing productivity, and helping employees manage expanding workloads. For their part, corporate employees have found that being able to work at home—even part-time—can increase productivity and job satisfaction and significantly reduce the burden of juggling professional and personal responsibilities.

In addition, many people—from baby boomers dissatisfied with traditional office jobs to retirees looking for ways to supplement income—are choosing to start businesses at home. This entrepreneurial bug has hit all segments of the population. In a recent Gallup poll, 80 percent of college seniors nationwide said they want to be entrepreneurs after graduation. For many of these men and women, a home office will provide an affordable and convenient headquarters. In fact, a study conducted by the National

Federation of Independent Business indicates that two out of three new businesses are started in the home.

Improvements in technology, specifically the Internet and phone services, make the home a viable office location. As the number of home-based businesses increases, the stigma of working with professionals who are home-based has diminished rapidly and is now rarely an impediment to doing business.

The home office has dramatically improved the quality of life for many people, but it also has its pitfalls. The convenience of a home office can lead to overwork and increased stress, and the distance between a home office and venues for social interaction can cause isolation. Limited interaction with peers and co-workers can leave some telecommuters and entrepreneurs feeling discouraged and unmotivated. The proximity of a household and family can increase pressures on people who are trying to excel at everything they do. If these factors are left unchecked, they can result in work/life imbalance, burnout, and health and emotional problems.

Ironically, part of the pressure from working at home can come from the freedom that it provides. After a lifetime of school schedules and regimented work environments, full freedom to plan your day can be daunting. Even telecommuters who are continuing their existing job responsibilities and are only changing location can experience pressure from having to structure their office time for themselves.

But working in a home office does not have to lead to these problems. Telecommuters and home-based entrepreneurs can take precautions to ensure that they create a positive work environment and a manageable schedule that enables them to enjoy the benefits of the home office without suffering from its potential negative effects. All home-based workers can learn to stay motivated in the face of setbacks, be a good boss to themselves, avoid isolation, manage time and stress, and establish a routine that encourages rather than chips away at health and well-being.

The extraordinary thing about the habits or adjustments needed to create a positive experience for yourself in the home office is that they do not require huge shifts in your current behavior. Even the smallest change in the way you approach things in a home office can vastly improve your quality of life and your work.

In this book you will learn how to make your home office experience the best it can be. If you are just starting out in the home office, use this book to help you to avoid developing any bad habits. As an experienced home office worker, use the book to help you to make minor adjustments that will deliver major benefits.

Best of luck, and please write to me at abredin@bredinbi.com or c/o Tribune Media Services, 435 North Michigan Avenue, Suite 1500, Chicago, IL 60611. I welcome your comments, insights, and questions. I cannot answer all mail, but I value every piece of it.

PART ONE

Emotional Survival

Motivation and Distraction

People frequently remark to me that you must have to be extremely self-disciplined to work at home. But although it is true that working at home puts you somewhat in charge of your schedule, plenty of people who do not regard themselves as particularly disciplined are able to work efficiently and successfully at home. The key to working successfully in a home office is determining what motivates you and what causes you to become distracted from your work. Armed with this knowledge, you can capitalize on your natural tendencies to do your best work. Motivation doesn't have a magic elixir, but in this chapter you will learn how to focus more effortlessly on your work and banish distractions.

Motivation through Routine

If you ever worked full-time in an office, you probably had a morning routine that moved you quickly and as efficiently as possible from bed to work. You may have had similar routines for getting ready for school when you were younger. But when you work at home and no longer have to operate so rigidly—and when no one is around to notice when you get to your desk —it's easy to dawdle. You may sleep a little later, read the paper a little longer, drink an extra cup or two of coffee, and read a magazine article. If you have bills to pay, you may get those out of the way or make some calls related to the vacation you are planning, the dinner party you are throwing, or the work you are having done in the yard. The next thing you know, half the morning is gone. That is because you don't have a routine that keeps your personal life from inching into your home office.

Establishing Routines

The single best thing you can do to get motivated to work each day is to create a routine that transports you from your bed to your desk in a fairly disciplined manner. The way you do it will depend on your own style. Here are a few examples of routines that other people have adopted, followed by some tips for establishing your own.

Steven runs a successful editing and copywriting business from his New York City apartment. When he first started freelancing, he adapted his former go-to-work ritual to create a clearly delineated beginning to his day. He did this by creating a reason to leave the apartment daily so that when he walked back in, he was officially "at work." Sometimes he'd go out for a muffin and coffee, other days he walked his daughter to day care. Still others, he walked the family dog around the block. The common ground with all of his routines is that in each he got dressed, left the apartment, and returned a short time later prepared to get to work.

Lori has been running a successful catering service out of her Long Beach, California, kitchen for six years. At first she had problems lighting a fire under herself to get to work each day. But after trial and error, she determined how to motivate herself. She discovered that if she didn't look good, she couldn't focus on her work. "I don't feel ready to work until I'm showered, dressed, and have my makeup on," she said. Her solution was to adopt a morning grooming routine as robust as the one she had when she worked outside of the house. Only after completing all of her primping, did she feel ready to head to the kitchen and begin her work.

Different routines motivate each of us. In order to determine what will help you, take note of those days when you get right down to work and cut through your list of tasks. Finding the best routine for your day may take some trial and error. Try the suggestions here to get started on finding your optimum routine.

- Set strict starting times for your day, and regard those times as inflexible.

- Have a set time to wake up each morning, and stick to it.

- Establish a clear boundary or ritual that marks the beginning of work every day, similar to the way Steven and Lori did.

- The next time you start the day with verve and stick to your schedule, take note of what was different about your routine.

- Get in the habit of letting unfinished personal projects wait until you have a break in your work schedule.

- Set up early morning conference calls, meetings, or other events that will help you start the day productively. If you find yourself having difficulty returning to work after lunch, do the same for the afternoon.

- Make a to-do list in the evening, and use it to keep you focused on work the next day.

- If you lack oomph in the morning, make phone calls to energize yourself or find another aspect of your work that infuses you with energy and start your day with it.

- Get into the habit of creating a short list each morning of the three things you need to accomplish during the day. Use this list to get you moving.

What Undermines Motivation?

Once you've found a routine that works for you, and you are at your desk ready to work on a predictable basis, you're halfway there. But being in the right place at the right time doesn't always guarantee that you will be eager to tackle the tasks at hand. Sometimes the will to work remains elusive. In order to find out what causes a lack of motivation, I talked to a group of psychologists. Look for something that sounds familiar to you in the following ten reasons.

1. Fear of failure is the cause of more work avoidance than laziness or distraction ever could be. And it can be especially scary when you are working on your own at home. If you're a telecommuter, you may dread the day your boss concludes that you should return to the office, and this fear may stop you from working in case a mistake you make will seal your fate. If you're self-employed, failure can be a make-or-break proposition. Maybe you heard this growing up and never thought much about it, but the reality is that we only fail when we're too afraid to try at all. The chances that you actually will fail are much slimmer when you do your best than when you allow the fear to take over.

Simply realizing that this is your fear may help the feelings dissipate. In addition, you can help yourself cope with fear of failure by imagining the worst outcome possible. If you can come to terms with its occurrence and realize that you can survive it, your fear will dissipate.

2. Fear of success is more often unconscious, but it can affect your motivation in a powerful way. If you would consciously like to build your business overseas, but at a deeper level worry about all the flying or about being separated from your family, your subconscious is really pulling for the status quo. Or if you telecommute, you may fear being in charge of your department or standing out from the crowd as an achiever because you fear you will lose friendships with co-workers as a result. Talking these concerns out with a friend or counselor will help you decide whether this is a problem you need to work on.

3. Boredom can crop up for a number of reasons, some more serious than others. If it's a routine task you can't avoid or can't hire someone to do for you (see chapter 5, Time Management), you have a number of tactics at your disposal.

▶ You can offer yourself a reward for doing it—for example, call a friend, read a chapter in your novel, go to the local café for some conversation and coffee.

▶ You can coordinate the dull task with one of your favorite distractions, such as filing while listening to a favorite radio show.

▶ You can promise yourself you'll only do it for 30 minutes and then you get to do something else.

▶ You can focus on the outcome rather than the task.

However, if you're frequently bored by your work-at-home job or business, it's time to reevaluate what you're doing in the first place. Everyone feels bored from time to time, but if you are bored every day by everything you do, step back and reconsider what you are doing for a living.

4. **Distaste for the work** is an occasional fact of life. No matter how much you love your job or your business, there will always be the tasks— filling out expense reports comes to mind—that you'll never quite cozy up to. The cure for this problem is similar to the one for boredom—you must set up a positive reward system. Sometimes humans are similar to lab animals in that we respond to treats. So the next time you have to run through the maze in your cage and you don't really feel like doing it, make sure there's a little piece of cheese waiting for you at the end.

5. **Uncertainty about how to do the task** is a special concern. If you are working in an office, you can ask someone nearby for help or you can brainstorm for ideas on how to begin a daunting project. All of these techniques can be done without making a formal request for help. But when you work at home, you may not have such easy access to advice. As a telecommuter you may be reluctant to call someone at the office to ask for help. If you are an entrepreneur, you simply may not know where to turn. In either case, the only way to deal with this situation is to encourage yourself to seek some help when you need it.

If you are a telecommuter, keep in mind that making contact with the office is part of keeping the lines of communication open. Your manager and co-workers should be glad that you are keeping in touch and exchanging ideas and asking for input. If you run a business, you need to remember that asking for help doesn't mean you lack the wherewithal to be successful. Visit the reference library, go to the bookstore, talk to peers, and contact business owners who have built businesses such as yours.

Many work-at-homers have found the Internet to be a great source of help and support. You can use the vast number of resources available on the World Wide Web to find new and different ways to tackle problems. And you can interact with like-minded individuals through Newsgroups and mailing lists. You may never meet some of these people face-to-face, but you may find yourself building a network you can call on when you need input or want to stay in touch.

6. Feeling overwhelmed by the project or job at hand is pretty common, and when you are in the grip of this uncertainty, you may find it difficult to start anything. If you are a telecommuter, break out of this trap by asking your peers or manager for help. Keep in mind that working at home doesn't mean you should expect yourself to solve all of your problems on your own. It should enhance your teamwork experience, not replace it. Whenever possible, enlist the help of another person for brainstorming. Jane, a documentary film producer, did this when she was having trouble starting a grant project that was due in two months. Instead of getting down to business, she was frittering away time that she could ill afford to waste. Jane got more and more panicky about her deadline, but nothing she said to scare herself into working seemed to help. She finally talked the problem over with a friend from graduate school and realized she was unable to start because she felt dwarfed by a gargantuan project. Together, Jane and her friend worked out a plan of attack, and the next day Jane was off and running on a series of tasks that would eventually add up to completion of her project.

7. Uncertainty about what to do next means you've lost sight of, or were never clear on, your goals. This dilemma can be solved by stepping back for a few minutes and thinking about what you intend to achieve in the longer run. If stepping back and thinking larger thoughts doesn't help you sort things out, don't be afraid to ask for guidance. If you are a telecommuter, ask your manager for help. Remember that asking for help does not mean that your telecommuting is a flop. Business owners don't have managers to turn to, but you may have peers, friends, or a mentor who can help you determine what your next step should be. If you must figure things out on your own, stand back from the project, literally and figuratively. Move away from your desk and your computer, pull out a pad of paper, and draw up a plan of attack. Start listing some of the tasks that you know are necessary to complete the project. The approach you come up with may not be perfect, but it will get you started. Breaking a job down into a series of tasks suddenly transforms it from overwhelming to fairly manageable.

8. Lack of structure means that you don't have a clear beginning and end to the workday, and that you are pretty uncertain about what you should be doing in between. As I talked about earlier, building helpful routines and creating structure is the foundation for working successfully at home. There are more techniques for scheduling and structuring time in Part Two of this book—Managing Time and Workload.

9. Lack of sleep, food, and exercise is among the most insidious culprits that steal energy and motivation from our days. When you are too busy to stop for lunch and then find yourself low on energy and snapping at people because you're irritable, or making a mistake because you're light-headed, you haven't done yourself any favor by skipping the meal. Also, skimping on sleep is a time-stealer in the long run. If you do it very often, you'll wind up exhausted and less than optimally productive. The time you save by getting up earlier or staying up late may be so unproductive that you don't save any time at all.

Exercise—and at the moment we're only talking about enough to clear your head and get your blood moving—is also critical to peak work performance. If you're sitting at the keyboard and can't seem to concentrate, your body may be trying to tell you something. You should stand up and stretch for a few minutes out of every hour you spend at the computer. For every two hours, you should walk around a little and get some fresh air into your lungs. I discuss exercise, food, and sleep in much greater detail in chapter 11, Exercise, Sleep, and Food.

10. Depression hits all of us from time to time and may last a day or two or even three—or longer. While it lingers, it can rob you of motivation. For simple depression brought about by overwork, outside events, or just the cyclical blues we're all prone to, try taking a long walk. Getting out and moving can be a big help because activity stimulates the nervous system and (depending on how fast and how far you go) can actually release endorphins, which activate the pleasure center in the brain. Chocolate does this, too, but its benefits aren't as long-lasting as exercise, and sugar also has a crash that accompanies it.

Sometimes depression is more serious and lasts longer than a few days. This is not a sign of weakness; rather, it's a treatable condition that you should talk to your doctor about. For some immediate feedback about whether what you are feeling could be chronic depression, take this standardized psychological questionnaire. Of course, only your doctor can diagnose the condition, but if you think you are depressed, you might want to take the completed quiz to the doctor's office. It could help you talk about how you've been feeling.

Depression is gradually becoming recognized for the common and treatable condition that it is. There is no evidence to indicate that people who work at home are any more likely to be depressed than are those who work outside the home. But depression is a common enough ailment to deserve attention in this book. If you've been feeling blue or low for more than a couple of weeks, you should talk to your doctor about how you're feeling.

The following quiz is known as the Wakefield Self-Report Questionnaire and is from an excellent book called *Depression and Its Treatment* by John H. Griest, M.D., and James W. Jefferson, M.D. (Warner Books 1992). The twelve simple questions will give you an idea about the level of your depression. Read these statements carefully, one at a time, and underline or circle the response that best indicates how you are. It is most important to indicate how you are now, not how you were or how you would hope to be.

1. I feel miserable and sad.

    (0) No, not at all
    (1) No, not much
    (2) Yes, sometimes
    (3) Yes, definitely

2. I find it easy to do the things I used to do.

    (0) Yes, definitely
    (1) Yes, sometimes
    (2) No, not much
    (3) No, not at all

3. I get very frightened or feel panicky for apparently no reason at all.

    (0) No, not at all
    (1) No, not much
    (2) Yes, sometimes
    (3) Yes, definitely

4. I have weeping spells, or feel like it.

    (0) No, not at all
    (1) No, not much
    (2) Yes, sometimes
    (3) Yes, definitely

5. I still enjoy the things I used to.

    (0) Yes, definitely
    (1) Yes, sometimes
    (2) No, not much
    (3) No, not at all

6. I am restless and can't keep still.

(0) No, not at all
(1) No, not much
(2) Yes, sometimes
(3) Yes, definitely

7. I go to sleep easily without sleeping tablets.

(0) Yes, definitely
(1) Yes, sometimes
(2) No, not much
(3) No, not at all

8. I feel anxious when I go out of the house on my own.

(0) No, not at all
(1) No, not much
(2) Yes, sometimes
(3) Yes, definitely

9. I have lost interest in things.

(0) No, not at all
(1) No, not much
(2) Yes, sometimes
(3) Yes, definitely

10. I get tired for no reason.

(0) No, not at all
(1) No, not much
(2) Yes, sometimes
(3) Yes, definitely

11. I am more irritable than usual.

(0) No, not at all
(1) No, not much
(2) Yes, sometimes
(3) Yes, definitely

12. I wake early and then sleep badly for the rest of the night.

(0) No, not at all
(1) No, not much
(2) Yes, sometimes
(3) Yes, definitely

Score the test by adding up the numbers you selected for each of the twelve items. Most depressed people tend to score above 14 on the test, whereas most nondepressed people score between 0 and 14. It's important to realize that a rating scale such as this does not diagnose clinical depression; it is only a measure of symptoms often associated with depression. It is likely that high scores may also be attained by individuals with other emotional problems or physical illnesses. Therefore, use the test as a guide, and consider consulting a doctor for an evaluation if your score is high.

Motivating by Goal Setting

After you've checked yourself over to determine why you are lacking motivation, it's time to draw on the biggest and best motivator of all: goal setting. Barry Farber is president of Farber Training Systems and is one of the nation's leading sales gurus. He's also author of *Diamond in the Rough,* a book of motivational techniques used by high achievers. He maintains that without a goal or mission, you aren't being pulled forward and you will consequently be at a loss for motivation.

Here is Farber's step-by-step technique for getting on track and staying focused in pursuit of your goals.

- Get out a few sheets of paper.
- At the top of the first sheet, write "My Goals for the Next 12 Months."
- Underneath that, write ten specific goals. They can be personal or professional—everything from earning more money to reading certain books, to getting more exercise.
- Pick the one goal in ten that will have the greatest impact on your life.
- Put that goal at the top of another page.
- Under that, jot down the question of how to achieve it; for example, "How can I make $50,000 more a year?"
- Next, list twenty actions that will get you closer to the goal — from making certain phone calls to attending more sales briefings.
- The final part of the exercise is to pick one of the twenty action items and do it in the next five minutes. And so on, choosing an action you can complete in the amount of time you have available.

Corraling Distractions

Let's say you began the day on time and pounced on your to-do list with great determination, but as the day wore on, distractions began to jostle for your attention. How do you get back on track when you find yourself peeking into the refrigerator every half-hour, reading the newspaper, answering e-mail from friends, doing laundry, framing an old photograph, or running to the store? Psychologists recommend using visualization. Imagine yourself as a train, moving toward the station; those distractions are a series of derailments, taking up precious time and keeping you from your true destination.

Another recommended technique is known as *Boundary Management.* Dr. Larney Gump, a professor of psychology at American University in Washington, D.C., and a clinician in private practice, suggests creating boundaries using time, activities, and space.

Time

In addition to being a resource that is ours to use any way we choose, time happens to come packaged as a highly limited quantity. The half-hour you spend daydreaming out the window or flipping through TV channels is gone, walled off from your use in a way that no other commodity can be. If you waste money, you can always earn more. But if you waste time, you can't get it back. Thus, thinking of time as having clear boundaries can reduce your vulnerability to the distractions all around you at home. One client Dr. Gump worked with a few years ago used to feel little motivation to start work each day until he figured out how much he could earn in an hour. Once the client did the math, he realized that every hour spent doing something directly related to getting clients or customers was worth $80. Therefore, when he spent the morning exploring the Internet, poring over the racing form, or puttering in his workshop, he knew he'd forfeited roughly $300—and because he'd never get back the time, that was $300 he'd missed out on forever. Once this connection was firmly established, Dr. Gump's client had all the motivation he needed to work first and play later.

Activity

Make up a company policy for yourself in which certain activities are not permitted during work hours. This type of boundary is helpful if you're tempted to leaf through the catalogs, play computer solitaire, or turn on the television set. You'll be less likely to give in knowing company policy forbids indulging yourself during designated work times. This technique is also part of creating and sticking to a schedule for your day. This may sound too contrived to be plausible, but much behavior modification is made up of tricks and techniques like these.

Space

This will be harder to do if you're operating out of an efficiency apartment, but if you can, create a boundary around your work area. For instance, if you're at your desk, you might not want to permit yourself to pay personal bills, chat with your family, or make personal phone calls. With clearly marked spatial boundaries, you'll find it easier to sort out the jumble of stimuli that come at you.

A useful way of thinking about distraction is to look at the word literally. Dr. Gordon Simerson, an associate professor of industrial/organization psychology at the University of New Haven in Connecticut, makes the point that the opposite of distraction is traction. "Feeling a sense of traction means that you've got a grip on what you're doing. There's a sense of momentum and engagement." Dr. Simerson says that if you're really engaged by your work, "you have a sense of flow and lose sense of the guideposts of moment-to-moment anxiety; you lose track of time, noises and events going on around you." So when you have traction, you're more protected from distraction.

Self-supervision

The space/activity/time Boundary Method effectively acts as a substitute for an immediate supervisor. This way you get the best of both worlds: you still make all the decisions yourself, but with the Boundary Method, you have something akin to a supervisor looking over your shoulder.

If you've been feeling unmotivated for a while and aren't sure why, ask yourself these five questions. The answers may help you figure out how to get back on track:

1. When was the last time you felt motivated?

2. What were you working on?

3. What was it about what you were doing that engaged you?

4. At what point after that did you begin to lose motivation?

5. What is the thing you like least about your current work project?

Procrastination

Procrastination is a common fallback position for many of us because it's *almost* foolproof. If you dither around with enough distractions and wait long enough, you no longer have the luxury of wasting time. The question of when to start work or whether to leaf through a magazine becomes academic. Once we're panicked enough, most of us manage to buckle down. But the problem with this schedule is that doing your best is tough when there's barely enough time to get the job done. Completing a project in a thoughtful and creative way with attention to detail isn't always possible if you've used the procrastination method to get yourself going.

Max, a telecommuter for a midsize software development company, uses procrastination to get himself going, "but only for jobs I really don't want to tackle. I procrastinate until I'm under deadline and have no choice but to get to work. For stuff I'm working on and excited about, it's not an issue." For large projects, or for those he's a little bored with, Max shifts his attention between two or three jobs during the day. He refers to this as "multitasking," which he says helps him procrastinate less and sustain motivation longer.

Tapping Your Motivation Source

We've talked about the common causes of low motivation and some ways around them. Now it's time to look at your natural abilities and inclinations and learn how to get them working for you. Everyone works differently, and being conscious of your personal preferences will do wonders for your productivity and sense of well-being. Focusing on your likes, dislikes, and unconscious tendencies will help you tap into what motivates you in both the short and long term.

There are no wrong answers to the following questions. The idea behind answering them is to become familiar with your own patterns so that you work the way that suits you best and feels most comfortable.

What time of day do you feel most energetic? Take advantage of your high-energy times to tackle your toughest or most challenging jobs. If this energy spurt occurs at 8:00 in the evening, plan your day around it. If you're a morning person, get up early and sit right down at your desk, before you shower and dress. The great thing about working at home is that you don't have to look good to do good work.

Are you truly a person who works best under pressure? Or do you just wind up working that way because you torment yourself with procrastination? If you can honestly say that the quality of your work doesn't suffer, then by all means use the incentive of a looming deadline to get going. If, after examining your conscience closely, you conclude that procrastinating hampers your best work, make it a goal to start early and avoid the last-minute rush.

Which do you prefer? To do the most appealing work first and then move on to the less compelling tasks? Or are you more likely to stay motivated if you know you'll have the reward of pleasant work after you do the worst? Learn which method fits you, and work in sync with your own style.

What do you like best about your work? Least? Give it some thought so that when you find yourself tempted by distractions, you can recognize that you're just putting off something you don't want to do. When you put your finger on that fact early, you'll be able to redirect your energies before wasting a lot of time.

Who would you rather go up against—a professional competitor or yourself? If you get your thrill from outdoing the business across town, then use that goal as an incentive. But perhaps you're daunted by the idea of a one-on-one challenge and you'd prefer to compete only with your own best efforts. Identify your preferences, and use them to propel yourself forward.

There are no right or wrong answers to the five questions above, so you don't need to score yourself. But you may want to write down your responses and check them from time to time to see if you've changed. Also, if you have trouble deciding which answer applies to you, start writing. Don't worry about style or punctuation; no one but you ever need see what you've written. But you'll be amazed at how putting your thoughts down on paper helps you clarify your ideas.

For the past two years, Dan has successfully telecommuted for his job as a software analyst with a major airline. At first he had a little trouble getting used to the unstructured environment, but said everything began to flow more smoothly when he learned something important about himself: "I hate the idea that I absolutely have to do something. It must be left over from childhood or something, but I can never bring myself to do anything if I think I'm under compulsion of any kind. So I learned the hard way to give myself the freedom to do a thing or not." Dan said he even used this method to quit smoking ten years ago: "I kept telling myself that if I really couldn't stand it, I could light up a cigarette. Just having that choice allowed me to *not* reach for the smoke. I use much the same approach to do my work. Maybe I'm perverse—but it works for me!"

A Note on Distractions vs. Other Activities

Spending time away from work purely for the purpose of avoiding certain tasks is not to be confused with enjoying movies, friends, or hobbies you engage in to have fun and refresh yourself. The immediate gratification of seeing a matinee or having lunch with a friend instead of, say, drafting the budget is likely to be followed by guilt, apprehension, or even self-disgust. You may find yourself feeling vaguely uneasy the whole time, as if dark clouds loom overhead. If gardening is your favorite pastime, it loses considerable zest and charm when you know you're supposed to be doing something else. You will save time and enjoy yourself more thoroughly in the long run by making sure that your time away from work is purposeful and pleasant instead of furtive and guilty.

Coping with Rejection and Setbacks

The Chinese have an interesting way of looking at rejection. Their character for "crisis" is the same as for the word "opportunity." They realized that when faced with a difficult situation, they had a unique chance to accomplish something significant. English doesn't have such a word with those dual meanings, but it would be great if we could firmly grasp that concept anyway. It's not possible to continually strive for bigger and better things without facing the occasional setback or rejection. The only way to avoid rejection consistently is to never try anything new, never push yourself. And, as you'll learn in this chapter, rejection and failure can be the gateway to accomplishment and success.

People who work at home as telecommuters or entrepreneurs need to possess this perspective. Without it, bad news in the form of a setback or rejection will derail you. Rejections and setbacks can throw anyone off track, but those of us working at home have the potential to be more dramatically affected by bad news because we are alone much of the time.

For example, if you experience rejections or setbacks when you work in a traditional office, you can share the bad news with co-workers and quickly gain perspective. Without those people around, you are likely to take the disappointing news more seriously and let it affect you more dramatically.

I have had a fair amount of firsthand experience with rejection. At one time or another I haven't measured up to someone's standard of writing, speaking, beauty, and a whole host of other things. I have also been fortunate to have some successes. Over time I have come to regard rejection as a part of my career, to expect a certain amount of it, and to not let it set me back. I have also learned how to turn it around and get something from it. I hope you'll feel the same way after reading this chapter.

> **I**f I had thought about it, I wouldn't have done the experiment. The literature was full of examples that said you can't do this.
>
> —Spencer Silver on his work leading to the invention of Post-it notepads.

Failure

Failure happens to everyone. Understanding that failure is part of life and business is the first step in learning to minimize its effect on you. Remember Coca-Cola's disastrous attempt to foist New Coke on the world? Or Microsoft's "Bob," the software with a happy-face symbol? Or that 1950s laughingstock, the Edsel, courtesy of Ford Motor Company? Even successful businesses like these with golden-touch images have blundered hugely. The key is that they step quietly over the corpse of their failures and sail serenely toward more successes.

To keep perspective the next time you fail, think of it this way: A baseball hitter is considered great when he bats .300—meaning that he gets a hit less than a third of the time he's at the plate. The other 70 percent of the time he fails. Yet he's a great hitter.

Following are eight specific recommendations for dealing with failure when it strikes you.

1. Remember that some failure is inevitable. If you think that every cold call must turn into a sale or that every person you deal with must be nice to you, you'll be suffering a lot of the time. Rejection happens; it is a normal part of life. In fact, you should expect to be rejected at least some of the time. That doesn't mean you should be negative or think, "Oh, what's the use?" It just means being realistic about the law of averages: If you're always out there, acting on your ideas, trying new things and taking chances, sometimes you're going to fail or get turned down. Writer Aldous Huxley once observed: "Experience is not what happens to a man; it is what a man does with what happens to him." Rejection is experience. It presents you with an opportunity to rise to the occasion and do something useful with it.

2. Don't globalize. To keep rejection from squishing your self-esteem, it's important not to blow failure out of proportion. My mother, who is a therapist, calls this globalizing—when you fail at one thing, you think that you are a failure at everything and that your life is awful. I'm lucky to have her to remind me not to do this. To avoid globalizing, make sure you do a reality check whenever you feel wounded by rejection.

3. Define success for yourself. What's your idea of success, and where did it come from? Many people think they've failed to achieve something when they never really wanted to do it in the first place. Maybe a father expected his daughter to be a doctor, or a wife thought that her husband should be company president, or your old friend from high school believed that big diamonds and flashy cars were the marks of a successful person. But if autonomy is more important to you than driving an expensive car, or if lavishing personal attention on your customers means more than boasting a client base three times larger than your current one, you could be succeeding beautifully on your own terms. Be sure you don't fault yourself for "failing" to achieve a certain standard of success that may not even be in your value system.

4. Don't suffer over rejection. We commonly think that the appropriate and inevitable reaction to rejection is to feel terrible. Not so. Rejection may be an objective fact. But the way you feel about it is completely subjective—and completely up to you. People and institutions have all kinds of reasons for rejecting you. Sometimes they have to do with you personally. Often they don't.

5. Talk about it. Working alone means that you're often facing rejection without the benefit of another person's perspective and sense of humor. These two elements are essential in a healthy rejection-coping mechanism, and this is where a solid professional support system really proves invaluable. You can always tell your best friend about a business disappointment and receive some sympathy. But no one will understand it better than another home-based colleague who's been there and might even have some tips based on his or her own experiences.

6. Celebrate rejection. When you remember what rejection means—that you've tried to accomplish something—you can begin to feel pretty good about it. In chapter 1, I referred to failure as a badge of honor, and that's not an exaggeration.

7. Read books about successful people. You will discover that many of the most prominent and accomplished people have experienced more setbacks and rejections than you and I fear we will in our worst nightmares. In 1962, the Beatles were told by one of the biggest record companies in the world: "We don't like your sound, and guitar music is on the way out." Winston Churchill was once at the bottom of his class at school. He was also repeatedly ridiculed and shunned in Parliament when he was warning against Hitler before World War II.

8. Stop worrying about what other people think of your failures. A friend of mine was recently upset because things were not progressing in her work the way she had hoped. One of her main concerns was that people would look at her as a failure and think that she was foolish for having set out on her course. I was sympathetic to her concerns, but I pointed out that anyone who looked down on her would actually be scorning her for pursuing something she was passionate about. If we boiled it down, she was worrying about the opinion of people who think it would be better to spend one's life not pursuing a dream but sticking to something safe and unfulfilling. By breaking it down like this, she realized two things: One, she was probably being harder on herself than most other people would be. Two, she didn't really care about the opinions of anyone who would disparage her for pursuing what she wanted.

How to Turn Rejection into Accomplishment

The type of rejection you face depends on the business you're in and, if you are a telecommuter, the culture of your company. Regardless of these details, it's safe to say that no matter what kind of rejection you experience, you can use the situation to propel you forward in some way.

Certain kinds of rejection teach you things about your skills. Others cause you to have an epiphany about the direction in which you are headed. If nothing else, rejection can sometimes give you a jolt of energy in the form of frustration and anger that you can channel into positive activities.

With this in mind, try an experiment the next time you fail: Try to make something out of the failure. The following suggestions provide some ideas for what you may be able to achieve.

▶ Focus on the things you did well, and find ways to build on your strengths. If you did a great presentation but the potential client went with another company because location was a factor, resolve to get in the door to do more presentations instead of sending proposals through the mail. If a colleague got a promotion because he or she interviews better than you do, but you produce better quality work, resolve to showcase your work more before the next interviewing process begins.

▶ Look as objectively as possible at the things you can do to improve. Ask family, friends, and colleagues you trust for their input.

▶ If you bid for a job and don't get it, survey your client to find out why. Take the person to a follow-up lunch, or send out a small postcard-size questionnaire. Your goal is to find out what the client saw in others that he or she didn't see in you. Ask questions to help figure out whether the reason was price, experience, quality concerns, or another factor that caused you to lose out on the business. You'll find, by the way, that people will be very honest if you tell them that you want the information so you can improve your services or learn more about ways to boost your business.

▶ Use the same idea if you lose a customer. Design a standard follow-up card that asks why the customer decided to go elsewhere. You will likely learn some useful things about how to improve your business. This also comes under the heading of good customer service. If you are a telecommuter and don't get a promotion you want, ask for feedback about why the job went to someone else. Ask your manager for help in developing a plan to build up the skills you will need to move ahead.

▶ If you think you've been rejected arbitrarily—and it happens—don't beat your head against the wall. Channel your frustration into work and turn it into determination to succeed despite the unfair treatment.

▶ Use the failure to build your resolve to succeed.

To get someone interested in a new idea, you must court rejection. Take a look at this example:

"So we went to Atari and said, 'Hey, we've got this amazing thing, even built with some of your parts, and what do you think about funding us? Or we'll give it to you. We just want to do it. Pay our salary, we'll come work for you.' And they said, 'No.' So then we went to Hewlett-Packard, and they said, 'Hey, we don't need you. You haven't got through college yet.'"

—Apple Computer founder Steve Jobs
on attempts to get Atari and H-P interested
in his and Steve Wozniak's famous Apple II

What would the world be like if Alexander Graham Bell had let these comments faze him?

"This 'telephone' has too many shortcomings to be seriously considered as a means of communication. The device is inherently of no value to us."

—Western Union internal memo, 1876

Getting in Shape

In order to be prepared to handle rejection when it comes—and to be able to risk rejection by taking chances—you must cultivate what management consultant and author Richard Koonce calls "emotional and psychological heartiness." To develop this strength, adopt habits and establish relationships that fill your emotional reservoir. These actions will help you build up life-affirming stamina that can help you easily get past rejection. For example, a day with my nieces and nephews adds to my emotional reservoir. They infuse me with their energy and creativity and provide a perspective on work.

To determine some steps you can take to cultivate your heartiness, read these tips below adapted from Koonce's book *Career Power! 12 Winning Habits to Get You from Where You Are to Where You Want to Be.*

1. Practice a little healthy selfishness by taking time out for yourself. This doesn't include time that you spend outside of work with family and social obligations, or life maintenance (such as cooking, unless it's a hobby). Spend pleasant time all by yourself with the idea that your sole objective is to recharge your batteries and come away feeling refreshed. This can be as simple as reading the paper leisurely, taking a hot bath, or listening to a favorite piece of music.

2. Never underestimate the power of friendships. Cultivate friendships. Friends are crucial when we need someone to talk to about a problem, but they are equally important to have around to share life's successes, too.

3. Find ways to help other people. This is an important aspect of living a balanced life. Whether you're doing well yourself or still struggling, look around for opportunities to lend a hand to another struggler. The psychological rewards will more than compensate your time and efforts.

4. Don't take yourself too seriously. If you already have a sense of humor or an ability to look at the world with bemused detachment, consider yourself blessed. If humor is not one of your natural gifts, you can cultivate this essential trait. When things seem bleak, deliberately look for the humor in the situation.

5. Make it a habit to think positively. Earlier I suggested that you expect rejection because it's inevitable. However, this is not license to stop believing that you can do whatever you set your mind to. To maintain a positive outlook, always keep your focus on what you want to accomplish, rather than on the reasons why it may not be possible. I used to have a quote (source unknown) on my desk that said "Nothing would be accomplished if all possible objections must first be overcome."

Setbacks vs. Rejection

A setback is any obstacle thrown in your path—for example, when your hard drive dies and you haven't backed up your files, when a trusted employee steals from you, when a fire destroys inventory, or when the economy works against your business just as you are getting on your feet. I recently heard a radio interview with a famous comedian who told of packing up and moving to Los Angeles after the owner of a comedy club told him he had talent and would put him onstage whenever he was in town. He and his wife quit their jobs and, when they arrived in L.A., went straight to the club—only to find it had burned down and was a smoldering pile of ashes. He didn't give up though, and now he is famous.

Although setbacks are generally less of an emotional blow than rejection is, they can pose a threat to your determination, particularly when you suffer several sequentially. The key to dealing with setbacks, as the following story makes painfully clear, is to expect them and prepare for them in advance as much as you possibly can.

Judy is a university instructor and also publishes a newsletter that is dear to her heart. Between those two jobs, Judy had virtually no personal life; she poured all her nonuniversity waking hours into the newsletter, which she hoped to turn into a full-time home business someday.

But Judy noticed that subscriptions were dropping off and wanted to find out why. One day she took advantage of an opportunity to have a marketing analysis class at the university survey current and former subscribers. The results that came back were somewhat harsh.

Criticism ranged from the quality of the articles and graphics to the occasionally erratic publication schedule. Judy was devastated: "I went for a walk the next day and almost started crying. It really stung and I began to fantasize about giving it all up and getting my life back." After all her hard work, it seemed that she was a failure as a newsletter publisher, and she felt personally rejected by her readers.

But today Judy continues to publish the newsletter and is working harder than ever to improve it with every issue. What happened? Judy credits good friends for helping her get through the painful time. "Being a home business and not having anyone immediately to talk to, you lose perspective," she said. "Fortunately, I have a wonderful support network of friends that I could turn to." But what made all the difference in the world, said Judy, were the comments of a couple of people. "Two or three people told me I was an inspiration to them and said they hoped I wouldn't quit. I don't make a lot of money, but I'm doing this because I want to make a difference. So when people tell me that I do, it makes it all worth it."

For perspective on rejection, read these letters received by famous authors, adapted from a wonderful little book, *Rotten Rejections* by Andre Bernard.

> *"Regret the American public is not interested in anything on China."*

(Pearl Buck's *The Good Earth,* the saga of the rise and fall of a Chinese peasant family, went on to win the Pulitzer Prize for literature in 1932 and become a best-seller.)

> *"Neither long enough for a serial nor short enough for a single story."*

(Arthur Conan Doyle's "Study in Scarlet" introduced Sherlock Holmes to the world.)

> *"I haven't really the foggiest idea about what the man is trying to say. . .a continual and unmitigated bore."*

(Joseph Heller's *Catch 22* not only added a phrase to our lexicon, but was an international best-seller and remains a classic of contemporary American literature.)

And if you've had a rejection that feels brutal to you, consider whether you'd rather get something as excruciatingly polite (and absurd) as this from a Chinese economic journal:

> We have read your manuscript with boundless delight. If we were to publish your paper, it would be impossible for us to publish any work of lower standard. And as it is unthinkable that in the next thousand years we shall see its equal, we are, to our regret, compelled to return your divine composition, and to beg you a thousand times to overlook our short sight and timidity.

Jeremy learned his lesson the hard way. He has an unglamorous but highly satisfactory and profitable business distributing seals and gaskets from his home office in Vermont. He's been in business for more than twenty years, but since 1994 he's done an increasingly large share o marketing through the World Wide Web and by sending out computer-generated faxes. His purchase orders arrive mainly the same way. "I loved my high-tech, low-shoe-leather setup," Jeremy said. "It was hard because I kept long hours and was pretty much a slave to my beeper. But it was also incredibly easy because I did 80 percent of the work without leaving home." In short, said Jeremy, "I was fat and happy."

He encouraged his customers to call him "Mr. Reliable" because he turned orders around so swiftly and consistently. It was an ideal arrangement until the Big Snowstorm of 1996 blacked electricity out in his region for four days and everything came to a standstill. No orders could come in, and no seals or gaskets could go out. "I was frantic because I could only take orders over my cell phone. And for those who needed something right away, I couldn't help them at all." Many of his frustrated customers, especially those who were not themselves victimized by the blizzard, were angry to find that "Mr. Reliable" had been completely stymied by the weather. Several went elsewhere, saying that they couldn't afford to use a supplier who could be out of commission at a moment's notice. "I'd say I lost at least a dozen lucrative customers," Jeremy said with a sigh.

Since that major setback, he has made a significant change in his business. Although he still depends on fax and e-mail for orders, Jeremy now sublets warehouse space in Arizona where he maintains backup inventory that can be dispatched to any point in the country in the event of an emergency. "I can't control the weather," he laughs, "but I found out I don't have to be at the mercy of it either."

Jeremy's story illustrates another key principle of setback prevention: Don't put all your eggs in one basket—or, in his case, all your gaskets in one basement. The next big snowstorm will be an inconvenience but not a disaster for his business.

Practical Tips for Preventing Setbacks

I recommend that you think of setbacks the way you think of heart attacks: Do everything possible to prevent them from happening. You can usually regroup and recover afterward, but preparing for setbacks will make the repair work much easier.

Here are some examples of actions you can take to block some of the most common setbacks. Only you know of others that are specific to your business, so use this list as a jump start and a reminder to start planning prevention now.

- Have technical support lined up and ready to call in an instant if anything goes haywire with your computer or other equipment vital to your business. And don't keep the technical support numbers in your computer files . . . because you won't be able to access them should your system crash.

- Have a backup supplier for your products for those occasions when your usual supplier gets snowed in, runs out of parts, goes out of business, and so forth.

- Computer accessories can and do give up suddenly at the most inconvenient times. At the very least, you should have an extra keyboard and mouse on hand in case yours gives out when you're on deadline. This may sound extravagant but it's really not. The best thing to do is upgrade from the mouse and keyboard that came with your original computer system. Then put the originals in the closet as backup. And, of course, always have an extra ink or toner cartridge on hand for your printer.

- Keep a cache of extra supplies in your closet. This way, when you're up late at night cramming for a presentation, you won't suddenly find yourself out of paper, folders, or letterhead.

- Invest in a good virus program for your computer—and make sure you keep it up to date with new viruses that appear regularly.

- Build in trouble time. When you're scheduling work, factor in a little extra time in case of setbacks. That way, if something unforeseen happens, you can recover and deliver your work as if all had gone smoothly.

- When you have to send a critical document or package, use a courier service that will allow you to track its progress as it goes. Or send it certified through the U.S. Postal Service, which gives you a receipt signed by the recipient.

- Don't rely too heavily on one client for your income. Make sure that you have lots of sources of income so that a setback in the form of a loss of a client will not destroy you financially.

▶ As a telecommuter, avoid relying completely on one employee or co-worker. Make sure you have lots of contacts in the office so that the loss of one co-worker won't sever your lifeline to the office.

▶ Have insurance. Some people believe that insurance is a waste of money, but I like it for peace of mind. If you are the breadwinner in your family, be sure that you have insurance that will provide income for your family if you are temporarily unable to work.

▶ Always job search. If you are a telecommuter, make sure your home-based status doesn't cause you to lose touch with recruiters and peers in your industry.

How's this for a setback? When Mrs. Debbi Fields took her recipe and her delicious idea to a group of investors, she was told: "A cookie store is a bad idea. Besides, the market research reports say America likes crispy cookies, not soft and chewy like you make."

When you do experience a setback, use the occasion to analyze what went wrong.

Ask yourself, "If I could turn the clock back three weeks, what would I do differently?"

▶ Did I research enough?

▶ Did I devote enough time to do the best possible work?

▶ Did I give the customer/manager enough opportunity to have input?

▶ Is there an opportunity to turn this setback into a success? If I've been turned down, what are my other options?

Evaluating Setbacks: Do You Really Have a Problem?

There are the times when a setback isn't really a setback. More often than you would imagine, business people perceive a setback when it is not really there. Hoboken, New Jersey--based publicist and professional organizer Ilise Benun included the following invaluable chart in her newsletter, *The Art of Self Promotion*. The scenarios are sales-oriented but apply to any business situation whether you are a telecommuter or a home-based entrepreneur.

What They Say	What You Hear	What They Mean	What to Do
I have a project; could you send your information?	They want me.	They're gathering info on potential candidates.	Send or fax your info; follow up in a week.
I'm sure it's on my desk somewhere. I haven't had time to look at it yet.	They don't want me.	Other things have come up and the project isn't quite as urgent.	Ask when to call back.
I've looked over your materials and they look interesting, but we haven't decided yet what direction to take. We'll be in touch.	They don't like it *or* they chose someone else	They're still strategizing.	Ask when they'll be making a decision.
The project is on indefinite hold. We'll be in touch if we decide to resurrect it.	They chose someone else.	Things have changed. This project isn't as important anymore.	Keep in touch about other possible projects.
Nothing; no call back.	They chose someone else.	They're busy with other things, or maybe they did choose someone else. It's not the end of the world.	Keep in touch every few months by fax, mail, and phone.

Humor

I mentioned earlier the importance of not taking yourself too seriously. What I want to do now is to persuade you to laugh as often as possible. Not only is laughing good for your physical health, it is also crucial to surviving setbacks and rejections with your self-esteem intact.

I'm not talking here mainly about jokes—Did you hear the one about the guy who walked into a bar dressed in a paper cowboy outfit? They arrested him later for rustling. That one may make you smile, but it's not going to do much for you when a project you want to manage goes to a co-worker or when a treasured client takes its business elsewhere. The kind of humor I am referring to involves cultivating a genuine sense of humor —the ability to find humor and absurdity in most situations, especially the most bleak. This story told to me by a friend is a good illustration.

Many years ago her father was in a coma, dying in the hospital. The entire family stood around his bed and most were sobbing, unable to speak. Suddenly, her sister choked back tears and came out with something their father loved to say at difficult moments: "You know, someday we'll look back at this and laugh!" Well, of course they wouldn't. But the absurdity— and bravery—of her sister's strangely timed joke broke the sheer misery of the moment. They spent the rest of their time in the hospital looking back with fondness and laughter, celebrating her father's life.

This brand of outrageous humor can do the same for you. Just when things look really awful and you feel as if you're staring into the face of defeat, humor can put you back on top of the situation. You're never really powerless if you can find a reason to laugh. As humor and health expert Alan Klein puts it, "You may not be able to change a situation, but with humor you can change your attitude about it. As a result of this new vantage point, you may also see new ways to deal with the problems."

Overcoming Isolation

3

U ninterrupted worktime and peace and quiet are two of the home office's greatest benefits, but they can also be the biggest downside of working at home.

No matter how much you enjoy the independence of working at home, too much time spent alone can be too much of a good thing. Hours of work, uninterrupted by conversations, calls, lunches, or other meetings with people, can leave you feeling less productive and hampered creatively. I learned this firsthand when my husband and I lived on the coast of Maine for two years. I had the most extraordinary view from my office window, and the woods surrounding our house could not have created a more peaceful environment for working. I marveled at the beauty and enjoyed the silence, but the isolation at times affected my energy and my mood.

To maintain energy levels and a high level of enthusiasm in a home office, you must employ some techniques for making sure you get the social contact we all need to feel vital. I'll be sharing insights and tips with you in this chapter for how to accomplish this.

Isolation—It Comes with the Territory

It's not uncommon for isolation to be an issue when you first start working at home. The progression usually goes something like this. For the first few weeks or months, you will love the peace and quiet and revel in the ability to accomplish more than is possible in most other offices. Then slowly, you will start to want more. After a productive stint at your desk, you will yearn for a chance to talk to a co-worker, visit someone else's office, have contact of some kind. If you do not satisfy your craving for contact, these vague desires can give way to feelings of loneliness, alienation, and even depression. The way you handle your isolation can make or break you as a home office worker.

If you are just starting a home business or you're thinking about telecommuting, give some thought to how much you like to be at home by yourself. Be realistic in looking at the amount of time you'll spend alone. But also remember that one of the great things about working at home is that you have the flexibility to set up your alone times and your social times almost any way you like. The key is to find the balance that works for you.

You're Not Alone in Feeling Alone

We all have varying levels of tolerance for solitude, but everyone needs some social interaction to keep a healthy mental balance. When you work at home, you need to determine how much contact you need and then make a plan for getting it.

A *Home Office Computing* survey of newly minted entrepreneurs revealed that a third of them longed for the casual camaraderie they used to have with co-workers. This was followed by 27 percent who missed having the backup support of office personnel such as assistants, secretaries, technical help, and so forth. Fully 15 percent of voluntary solo practitioners said they missed being part of a team. None of these responses suggest that entrepreneurs regretted their choice to work at home. The statistics simply indicate that the respondents missed certain things about working in an office and that they need to find ways of replacing them.

The switch from a corporate to a home office does indeed remove many valuable interactions you might previously have taken for granted. Simple daily exchanges with co-workers such as "How was your vacation?" "How about that Knicks game?" or "My sister had her baby!" go a long way toward making us feel connected with the world. Add to that both the opportunity to discuss ideas and problems with colleagues and the proximity of a supervisor who can give you direction, guidance, or praise when you need it.

It is possible to discover highly satisfactory substitutes for all of these. What you wind up with may depend on where you live. If you're in the midst of an urban environment, you may have the easiest time. You can walk a block or so to a coffeehouse where you see familiar folks with whom you can chat as you open your mail. If you live in the suburbs, interaction with others becomes slightly more difficult. You may need to book a lunch appointment with a friend, or even cultivate your local merchants so you can at least greet them by name and exchange a few friendly words as you make your rounds. When you're located in a rural area, you face a more challenging situation. When even the closest grocery store is a half-hour drive away, casual daily contact may not be easy to come by. You may need to spend more time on the telephone and with your e-mail buddies just to get a daily "fix" of casual camaraderie.

Isolation vs. Solitude

This distinction is key. Solitude is time spent alone, which can be a refreshing and creative experience. But if solitude goes on too long, you begin to feel cut off from the rest of the world. When this happens, the serenity of solitude gives way to the loneliness of isolation.

Some of us "recharge our batteries" by spending time alone. If that describes you, your tolerance for solitude is much greater than someone who feels most energized when in the company of others. It's important to know your own style and comfort level because your need for socialization versus solitude can determine whether you thrive or shrivel as a home-based worker. Let's begin by figuring out where you fall on the introvert/extrovert scale.

Are You an Introvert or an Extrovert?

Both strong introverts and strong extroverts will have some difficulty adapting to working from home. Take this quiz to determine where you fall on the introvert-extrovert scale.

Answer the questions below, rating how well each statement describes you. At the end of the test, add up your score and read the comments that pertain to the type you most closely resemble. *Score:* rarely, 1; sometimes, 2; frequently, 3; always, 4.

1.	I turn on the TV as soon as I get home.	1	2	3	4
2.	I do my best work with others around.	1	2	3	4
3.	Time goes more quickly for me when I'm with others.	1	2	3	4
4.	I'd rather walk in the city than in the woods.	1	2	3	4
5.	I get easily bored on my own.	1	2	3	4
6.	I'd rather go to a party than spend the evening at home.	1	2	3	4
7.	I feel restless after a whole day spent alone.	1	2	3	4
8.	I don't like to eat alone.	1	2	3	4
9.	I get a lot of energy from being around people.	1	2	3	4
10.	I need friends or colleagues to problem-solve.	1	2	3	4
11.	Frequent feedback helps me enjoy working on a project.	1	2	3	4
12.	When things go wrong, I call a friend right away to talk.	1	2	3	4

Your score:

12–20 Strong introvert. You probably need to get out more than you're doing now. It's likely that certain critical aspects of your business such as marketing and networking are loathsome chores to you. Make a disciplined effort to incorporate the long- and short-term strategies for breaking isolation, and you stand a good chance of learning to enjoy interactions that are critical to the success of your business. Be careful that you don't substitute computer games for social contact.

21–30 Moderate introvert. You probably don't have much problem coping with the relative isolation of working at home. But chances are that you're not in sales and that you also have trouble networking on a regular basis. Make regular interaction breaks a priority, and adopt at least one long-term isolation buster from this chapter.

30-35 Introvert/extrovert. You enjoy solitary and social time in a fairly balanced way. You have trouble with isolation when a deadline or major project keeps you from your usual regime of socializing. Make a note of the quick isolation busters in this chapter, and keep them handy for these occasions.

36–41 Moderate extrovert. It's easy for you to feel cooped up and lonely. But the good news is that you aren't likely to let that happen very often. As an extroverted person, you probably initiate contact whenever you feel you need it. Take special advantage of the quick tips for breaking isolation. These will help you get the stimulation you need frequently without losing much work time. Keep your schedule regular so that you don't get off track by using too many isolation busters.

42–48 Strong extrovert. You may have trouble handling the isolation that comes with working at home. Use both short- and long-term isolation busters as efficiently as possible to maximize contact and stimulation while getting work done. Pay close attention to how you feel every day, and schedule your work and break times carefully. Be careful of spending lots of time chatting on the telephone or hanging out with the mail deliverer or neighbors.

There is no hard-and-fast answer at this point about who will work well at home. The best I can tell you is that recent studies show that both strong introverts and strong extroverts will have some difficulty adapting to working from home. If this quiz puts you in either category, take it seriously and take advantage of all the tips in this chapter. Also, be cautious about the isolation traps listed at the end of this chapter.

Isolation among Corporate Telecommuters

Alienation can be as much of a problem as isolation for those who work for a large company but are away from daily contact with co-workers and bosses. If your company's telecommuting program doesn't have a carefully designed policy concerning communication with remote workers, ask for one. The bottom line is that there is no such thing as too much communication. You might want to try doing some of the following things:

▶ Regularly talk with your supervisor and co-workers to maintain good working relationships.

▶ Request weekly team teleconferences.

▶ Suggest meeting in person whenever possible.

▶ Make sure you get copied on all memos and e-mails that go to your area.

▶ Set up a buddy system so your office buddy can keep you posted on daily office news, memos, and other relevant goings-on.

Remember that as a telecommuter, you are tethered twice. First, you're at home and therefore more isolated than most of the workaday world. Second, you're *not* in the office, which is sometimes luxurious and sometimes isolating. By following these four dos and don'ts, you may find yourself more in sync with the goings-on in your office.

1. Don't miss office parties; by attending, you show that you're still one of the crowd.

2. Do have lunch with a colleague at least once every two weeks. These don't have to be working lunches, just a chance to catch up with a co-worker.

3. Do let co-workers know if you are feeling isolated. They will probably make an effort to call you more regularly.

4. Do make sure you attend all going-away parties, baby showers, soft-
   ball games, and other activities that will keep you in touch with the
   office.

One telecommuter told me that he occasionally felt the way he did in second grade when he was quarantined at home with chicken pox. Then it seemed as if everyone in the world was outside playing and having fun while he was stuck inside. He enjoyed his telecommuting status for the most part, but whenever he felt like he "had chicken pox," he'd call a co-worker and set up a lunch, or just drop into the office for a day and do his work there.

Warning Signs of Isolation

The signals that tell you you've been alone too long are highly individual. They range from relatively minor signs that you should be getting out more

You know you've been alone too long when . . .

Dixie Darr, publisher of the *Accidental Entrepreneur Newsletter*, came up with these tongue-in-cheek-but-grain-of-truth symptoms of isolation:

- You get upset when the mail arrives late.

- You're ultrafriendly at the post office, dry cleaner, grocery store, etc.

- You become a regular caller to talk radio.

- You don't want to go anyplace where you have to wear
  shoes.

- You realize it's been three days since you've talked to
  anyone but your cat.

- Your cat starts answering you.

to serious symptoms such as depression and alienation. Look over this list, and check the signs that apply to you. Ask yourself if they coincide with spending more time alone. If they do, pay special attention to both the long- and short-term isolation-busting strategies suggested in this chapter.

- ▶ You are snacking more and enjoying it less.
- ▶ You're feeling less energetic than usual.
- ▶ Your creativity seems blocked.
- ▶ You're feeling more stress lately.
- ▶ You catch yourself being impatient and judgmental toward others.
- ▶ You feel bored a lot of the time, even when there's plenty of work to do.
- ▶ You frequently feel alienated from the world around you.
- ▶ Your pantry is low because you aren't shopping regularly.
- ▶ You haven't bought any new clothes in six months or longer.
- ▶ You're running up credit card bills because you're shopping just to do something other than work.
- ▶ You notice that you aren't up-to-date on new trends or technology in your field.
- ▶ You feel less able to express yourself articulately.
- ▶ You feel restless much of the day.

Seven or more check marks may indicate that you're in the grip of long-term isolation. Make a pact with yourself to get involved in one of the long-term isolation buster suggestions. Also, work on at least one short-term isolation buster every single day.

Isolation Busters

It's natural to feel isolated when you work by yourself. It doesn't mean that you're failing or that your situation is not working out. It simply means that you need to make some changes in the way you structure your day. Part of what keeps people from finding solutions to their problems with isolation is that they believe they will have to make radical changes to improve their situation. But this is not the case. Take a look at these short- and long-term isolation busters, and pick a few that will work for you.

Short-term Isolation Busters

No matter how busy you are, you can work any of these quick tips into your day:

1. Reach out and touch someone. . .

▶ Use e-mail to keep in touch with friends and colleagues. If you can't call (or don't have time), electronic messages will maintain your connection and help you feel less cut off.

▶ Pick up the telephone to call someone you can really talk to. There's nothing like a satisfying conversation with a close friend. Just ten to fifteen minutes on the telephone can make you feel like a member of the world again.

▶ Make a telephone lunch date—eat your sandwich while you chat on the phone with a friend. Just because you can't go out for lunch doesn't mean you have to eat alone.

2. Get moving.

▶ Take a ten-minute walk. Even if you don't talk to another soul, you are out in the world and no longer alone.

▶ Run an errand. This also gets you out in the world and will give you the chance to talk briefly with other people.

▶ Patronize local businesses and learn the names of the people you deal with. You'd be surprised at how much lift you can get from a personal exchange with the people you see regularly. I know one person who refers to his local Mail Boxes Etc. as his "general store for home office workers," because everyone who works alone in the neighborhood seems to congregate there to chat and catch up, just as one might at a small-town general store.

▶ Take scheduled breaks every hour—even if it's just to get up for a drink of water. Every psychologist I spoke with recommended this one. It may seem a little compulsive to schedule brief breaks—but if you don't schedule them, you won't take them. In the long run, it's a highly productive way to spend two or three minutes an hour.

3. Add soothing sounds.

▶ Sometimes silence is deafening. Listen to the radio at a very low level or leave the TV on in the background. If you keep the sound at a level where it doesn't break your concentration, the radio or TV can literally keep you company throughout the day.

▶ If you're lucky enough to play a musical instrument, sit down and play for a few minutes. Music will reduce your stress level and take your mind off feelings of isolation.

Long-term Isolation Busters

The short-term isolation busters are quick fixes and not substitutes for regular social contact. In fact, if you did a few of these each day but did nothing else, chances are you'd be feeling isolated before long. So be sure to employ at least one or two of the long-term isolation busters listed below.

1. Take a class that will expand your professional knowledge or personal horizons. This is a commitment of your own time. But it will pay dividends in giving you new ideas and insights in addition to helping you meet new people.

2. Teach a class or agree to give a talk. Both of these can be great public relations and a good way to meet like-minded people.

3. Organize a party or get-together. You'll have fun doing the planning and have something to look forward to in the future, and the party itself will be a great remedy for feeling isolated.

4. Join a professional organization or support group. This tactic has worked wonders for just about every home-based entrepreneur I know.

5. Have an informal board of advisers so that you can meet or speak regularly with a group of people whose judgment you trust. This can provide regular social contact, but more important, it can give you insight into your business that you wouldn't be able to get elsewhere.

6. Set up a collaboration or joint-project with a colleague you respect. This way you have the best of both worlds—working on your own, but having input and camaraderie from your partner.

7. Volunteer with a community agency to help other people. Sometimes when we feel most alone, the best thing to do is get out and help somebody else. Not only does it break your isolation, but the feeling you get from giving something to someone else is deeply satisfying.

8. Join a gym, a walking group, or other activity-oriented bunch, and participate regularly.

Networking

Networking is an important business strategy and a great way to counteract isolation. It's a term that gets lots of lip service, but I've noticed that many of us don't truly understand the concept and don't know how to network for maximum advantage.

Networking is much more than handing out your business card at parties and meetings. Effective networking is about building solid connections with a group of people who share similar goals and interests. Regular get-togethers with this group can be productive for your short- and long-term interests and a real asset to your business.

A good networking group can:

▶ Inspire you to go after your dreams—and then keep checking to make sure you're taking action on them.

▶ Help you brainstorm about business ideas.

▶ Give you tips on marketing, list-building, or any of the questions that come up for your business.

▶ Sympathize with your headaches while they share stories of how they themselves handled difficult situations or deadbeat clients.

In other words, a good networking group that you build selectively can become surrogate mentors, bosses or colleagues, or genuine friends—whatever the occasion calls for.

You can build your networking group on your own by utilizing your circle of professional and personal contacts. You might be meeting these like-minded individuals at industry conferences, Chamber of Commerce meetings, or even your kid's Little League game. Another option is to look into a professional networking group, a sort of matchmaking service for business owners. The company will put you together with five to ten other noncompeting business people, and your group will meet every month or so. Although you won't do business with the members of your networking group, you will get access to their lists of contacts, their expertise, and their support. Check with your Chamber of Commerce or look at ads in your local business journal to find these companies.

Remember that building your network is an evolutionary process. It's natural that you will have a richer and more satisfying group after two years of working at home than after two months.

Electronic Networking

One of the benefits of having access to the Internet is that you can extend your networking community much more broadly than you can with face-to-face networking. It gives you the ability to hook up with like-minded people who have interests similar to yours, and it lets you communicate with them no matter where they're located.

One of the easiest ways to do this is via the Usenet or newsgroups. The first thing to know about newsgroups is that they don't necessarily have anything to do with news. They are nothing more than special-interest discussion groups. And there are thousands of them, ranging from highly focused special interests such as "Users of Microsoft Excel for the Macintosh," to more general subjects such as "Small Business Entrepreneurship." There are also a wide range of groups that cover hobbies and interests—for example, jazz music, jewelry making, and amateur astronomy.

Several Internet search engines scan newsgroups; one of the better-known ones is DejaNews (http://www.dejanews.com). If you spot a topic that sparks your interest, you can subscribe to that newsgroup using the "news reader" that comes with your web browser. You'll then begin to read people's postings to the board. You can also post articles (replies or fresh thoughts) yourself, or respond to people privately via e-mail. In other words, you immediately become part of a community of people who have the same interests as you do.

Similar to newsgroups are Internet mailing lists, which are made up of groups of people who exchange e-mail on a subject that interests them. Instead of using your browser's news reader, you get e-mail sent directly to your box on the subject. Depending on the size of the list, you may find yourself getting anywhere from 10 to over 100 e-mails a day on the subject, so be prepared to check your e-mail box at least once a day. If you find yourself deluged by mail you can't read, you might want to read the list in digest format, where several days' worth of mail are sent in a single file that you can review at your leisure. To find mailing lists on topics that interest you, use Liszt.com, a World Wide Web–based directory of lists (http://www.liszt.com).

Some Perspective on Isolation

Peter Suedfeld is a psychology professor at the University of British Columbia who specializes in isolation studies. Although he believes that most people actually don't get enough solitude, he cautions against the dangers inherent in too much isolation for the home-based worker: "If you work in an office, you look for serenity. If you work at home, you must seek out social and recreation time."

According to Suedfeld, each of us has a "psychological thermostat" that causes us to seek either company or solitude, depending on what we need. This will be different with different people (see the introvert-extrovert quiz on page 38). Be sure to pay attention to your "thermostat" and take action when you're too cold (too much solitude) or too hot (too little time alone).

Take "Social" Breaks

The little breaks that are so vital to our productivity and mental health happen naturally in a traditional office. You leave your desk to send a fax, to photocopy a contract, to get a box of staples from the supply cabinet, or maybe to get a drink of water. These errands are commonplace activities. The huge difference is that when you perform them at work, you are likely to enjoy a little social break. You see Jill at the supply cabinet and hear about a movie she saw last night. At the photo copy machine, Pat tells you about his new dog. And so it goes.

But when you're at home, these trips for copies, water, staples, and so forth, only net you what you got up for. To overcome isolation and thrive on your own at home, you must create something that approximates bumping into one of your office pals at the watercooler.

Andy left a bustling corporate life to create his own credit management business at home. As a fairly introverted person, Andy thought he would love being alone at home. But for the first three months in his new environment, Andy missed the office atmosphere he'd left behind. "Sure, I talked on the telephone plenty," he recalled, "but sometimes I only saw the UPS and FedEx delivery people in the course of a day." As a single person, Andy had no one to share his triumphs or listen to his troubles at the end of a day.

After three months of wondering whether he'd made a mistake in leaving his corporate environment, Andy took action. He scheduled a tennis game every Tuesday and Thursday afternoon. Every Friday he met a former colleague for lunch. On the days he didn't play tennis, Andy took himself to a local bookstore or café just for a change of scenery and some casual conversation. "It made all the difference in the world to me," said Andy. "These few things really made me feel plugged into the world again." He began to concentrate better when he was at his desk, and he credits a breakthrough idea to chat sessions he had with a tennis partner as well as with his Friday lunch friend.

Extrovert Richard thrives on telecommuting from home as director of public relations for a law firm. Because he needs a fair amount of contact with people, Richard has arranged his schedule accordingly. One of the isolation busters he most enjoys is travel, often mixing business and pleasure. His work as a law-firm marketer requires frequent trips throughout North America. "But once or twice a year," he said, "I just feel like I need a change of scenery. I take my laptop and go to New York or Boston, or some other location where I have friends, a place to stay, and full computer access. I get my work done, maybe visit a client at my own initiative, visit old friends, and come back rejuvenated."

Isolation Traps

As entrepreneurs or even as telecommuters, we're a fairly independent bunch. This independence can lead us to recoil from things that look like an organization, because that's precisely what we have left behind. This kind of thinking—which I call "isolation traps"—can keep us from doing the very things we need to do to help ourselves.

Trap #1. "I'm not a joiner." An entrepreneurial group or network doesn't have to be more than a handful of people you hit it off with and can talk to comfortably. It may even be that the only thing you have in common with some of your network buddies is that you work at home in similar businesses.

Trap #2. "I don't need to brainstorm." Without feedback from friends or colleagues, we are only looking at a problem or situation from one point of view. In the long run, lack of this kind of interaction undercuts our creativity just as it impairs our perspective. No matter how creative or original we are, most of us need to talk with someone else who can help stimulate and clarify our ideas. This process generates new ideas, new slants on old ideas, and so forth.

Trap #3. "I shouldn't depend on others." Conscientious people have a strong tendency to be self-critical. If you are that way, you'll wind up denigrating your work, thinking it's less valuable, less interesting, and less important than it really is. You can lose confidence in what you're doing. All of this makes it very difficult to maintain the energy and confidence so vital to continuing your work.

Trap #4. "I'd rather not have to see people very often." If you tend toward introversion, be careful of this isolation trap. You may get carried away by the cozy feeling that you rarely have to leave the house and can conduct business by phone, fax, and e-mail. Giving way to this tendency can put you into a downward spiral that may result in depression. First, you don't get dressed all day; soon, you don't shower daily; eventually, you don't feel upbeat and you lose the desire to take on challenges. It's hard to feel competent, creative, and crisp when you're moping around in scruffy sweats and slippers. Business contacts will sense this, and you'll lose clients.

Being a Good Boss to Yourself 4

One of the chief benefits of working in a home office is the ability to be your own boss. However, if as a boss you lack the management skills, communications skills, and interpersonal skills to help yourself get the job done, you may actually be at a disadvantage. Whether you're an entrepreneur or a telecommuter, you are responsible for being a boss, employee, mentor, and trainee in your home office. If you don't exercise the proper management techniques, you'll find it difficult to motivate yourself and get the most out of your efforts.

Most successful companies are driven by people with vision, who can pass this vision on to their employees. People who work alone also need this type of vision, and they need to convince themselves that their vision is accurate and worth following. That's the essence of self-management. In this chapter, you'll learn what makes a good boss and how you can apply their techniques to managing yourself—from ways to stay positive, to the benefits of setting clear and attainable goals, to places you can go to get support when none seems available.

What Makes a Good Boss?

Before you begin to tackle the skills you'll need to be a good boss, you might want to take a minute to think about the characteristics you've most admired in the people you've worked for. I've listed the following winning ways, but you might want to jot down a few of your own.

A good boss motivates. They are able to get the most out of their staffs. They make people feel good about the project they're involved in, and let them know the importance of their contribution to the success of their team.

A good boss provides positive feedback. They know that negativism never works, but that positive language empowers. A pat on the back and the words "well done" or "good job" keep people engaged. They thank people for their contributions and acknowledge their accomplishments.

A good boss sets clear goals. They are explicit in what they expect from people. They see what needs to be accomplished and are crystal-clear on how to get there. Their goals are challenging yet attainable.

A good boss helps you improve yourself. They know that nobody is happy being stagnant. They see self-improvement as a positive thing, and they're not threatened by someone's growth. They give people the opportunity to learn new skills that make them a more valuable part of the team.

A good boss doesn't second-guess you. They trust your judgment, because they know that if they've given you responsibility, it is yours to own. They don't look over your shoulder and correct your every move. They're interested in the end—they don't care what route you take as long as you make it to the destination on time.

A good boss rewards you for a job well done. They know that they can't move forward on their own, and they share the rewards of success. They understand the true value of sincere praise, and they're able to clearly explain what you did to deserve that recognition.

A good boss gives you the tools you need to do your job. They know that you can't thrive in your job if you're handicapped by the wrong equipment or information. They understand the power of technology to save time and money and make you more efficient. They know that information is a competitive advantage, and they encourage you to learn as much as you can.

Now that you know what you like to see in a boss, you need to find a way to apply those techniques to yourself. It's not as easy as you might think, because most people are much harder on themselves than they are on others. That's why this chapter is about being a "good" boss. . .not a "tough" boss or a "demanding" boss. I've gathered up some self-management techniques that I've found to be successful, and I'll show you how to implement them in your home office.

The Real Power of Positive Thinking

Did you know that you're probably sending yourself negative, self-defeating, motivation-robbing messages all day long? Behavioral research asserts that up to 78 percent of everything we think is negative, counterproductive, or in some way self-defeating.

When you stop and pay attention to what goes on inside your head most of the day, you'll find that it's fairly self-critical. How many times do you actually say "I've never done this before but I know I can do it!" or "I'm getting closer to achieving my goals and ideals every single day"? Those sentences even sound a little weird.

What probably will sound less strange is the constant babble of worries, fears, self-doubt, and self-criticism that chatter inside our heads most of the time: "I'm terrible at marketing, and I hate doing it," "I never could do math, and this budget sure looks like it," and so on. Do these statements sound a little more familiar?

The constant repetition of these negatives has a strong effect on self-esteem. We become unmotivated, and our overall performance suffers. We take our successes for granted and constantly tell ourselves what we haven't done or haven't accomplished. Think about it this way: If you worked in a corporate office, and three-quarters of your boss's remarks to you were negative, you wouldn't want to work for this person very long. In fact, successful corporate managers are taught to explain everything with a positive slant—not "You're doing this wrong," but "Here's how you can do it right" or "Here's how you can do even better."

So, why do you need to put up with this kind of negative behavior when it comes from you? The answer, of course, is that you don't.

Turn Negatives into Positives

The first step toward being your own best boss is to take all your negative self-talk and turn it into positive, motivational speech. Here are some practical ways to do this:

Track your self-talk patterns. When do you talk to yourself, and when are you most negative? You might find yourself making excuses for not doing something, criticizing yourself for not being perfect, saying you can't do things when you're making a list. It is critical that you become aware of what you are doing and when you are doing it.

Make your self-talk specific. Many of the generalizations we make about ourselves are negative, and we use them as a way of invalidating our self-worth. But if we're specific, we can find a way to learn from our experiences. For example, instead of saying "I'm lazy," try to relate that to something specific you may have done, such as "I missed that deadline because I failed to pay attention to my schedule." Use the same strategy for positive self-talk because it always feels good to have someone enumerate your successes—"I really impressed them with this project because keeping to my deadlines made me clear in my objective."

Watch your language. It's quite common for people to be tough on themselves or to hedge their accomplishments. Look out for judgmental words such as "should" and turn them into more inspirational words such as "can"—"I should clean my desk" has highly negative connotations because it assumes you've done something wrong by being a bit messy, whereas "I can clean my desk" gives you the option and empowers you to do it. Banish "hopefully" and "maybe" from your vocabulary, because, well, you wouldn't want me to tell you now that "hopefully this advice will work for you."

Try the two-for-one exercise. Esther Bogin, director of people-management consulting firm People Communications in Dix Hills, New York, shared this one with me. She suggests that every time you tell yourself something that you have to do, or every time you get down on yourself for making a mistake, you should also make two positive statements about yourself. This gets you into the habit of being positive and quickly changes the ratio in favor of motivational language.

Treat yourself as well as you treat others. If a friend of yours came to you because she was frustrated with a project, wouldn't you try to encourage her and give her positive advice by telling her how talented and accomplished she is? Start saying the same things to yourself, because when you're in a virtual office, you often need to be your own best friend.

Affirmations

In his book, *What to Say When You Talk to Yourself,* Dr. Shad Helmstetter suggests affirmations for everything from stopping smoking to getting organized. He has a set aimed specifically at boosting self-motivation, although you can certainly come up with your own. The keys are to keep the affirmations in the first person, to keep them positive, and to be as specific as possible. Here are some examples:

- ▶ "I can do anything I set my mind to."

- ▶ "I am good at my job and am capable of handling every new problem that comes along."

- ▶ "I welcome problems, because solving them helps me get smarter and better all the time."

Dr. Helmstetter suggests making a list of affirmations and reading them into a tape recorder. You can then play them back when you're in the car, or during downtime at your desk, or whenever you need to remind yourself how important you are. By the way, if you have a problem getting used to hearing the sound of your own voice on tape, make overcoming that obstacle the goal of your first set of affirmations. If you think that affirmations are silly and don't lead to results, keep in mind that Scott Adams, creator of the Dilbert comic, used positive affirmations to reach his goal as a syndicated cartoonist.

Goal-Setting

Goal-setting is crucial to success in any business, but it's particularly important for home-based workers because they can become distracted without focus. Goals direct your actions, give you something to aim for, and can serve as a yardstick for measuring your success.

It's not only important to set goals, it's also important to document them by *writing them down*. I can't stress this enough. Putting your goals down on paper makes them real and commits you to them. If this process scares you, it may make you feel better to know that you're not alone—fewer than 5 percent of people write down goals or have action plans for attaining them. But don't give into this fear. Remember that a goal can be changed at any time after you write it down. Also keep in mind that goal-setting becomes easier the more times you undertake it. When you have set goals and attained them, the power of goal-setting will compel you to set more.

You also might want to share your goals with others. If you're a telecommuter, show your goals to your immediate supervisor to make sure you're on track with the direction of the company. If you're an entrepreneur, show them to a peer or friend who will be supportive, yet critical enough to call you on goals that don't pass muster.

It's essential to create a series of short- and long-term goals. You might want to set weekly goals, quarterly goals, annual goals, and even three-year or five-year goals. One way to generate short-term goals is to first consider your long-term goals and work backward. Is your goal to earn $100,000 this year? Then what do you have to do this quarter to attain this goal? It might be something such as "Add two new clients." Then turn that quarterly goal into weekly goals—"Make five marketing phone calls by Friday." See how it works?

The way in which you set goals strongly affects their effectiveness. Use these guidelines when you go through the process:

Be positive. As you saw earlier, it's easier to be negative about yourself than than it is to be positive. Bring your "positive thinking" techniques to your goals. "Do this well" is much better than "Don't make this mistake."

Make your goals measurable and precise. Use dates, times, and amounts so you can measure your achievement (and take satisfaction in knowing what you've accomplished). "Make more sales calls" is general and offers no way to gauge your success, but "Call eight prospects by June 15" is measurable because it has both an amount and a deadline.

Set performance, not outcome goals. Take care to set goals over which you have as much control as possible. If you base your goals on personal performance or skills or knowledge to be acquired, then you can keep control over the achievement and draw satisfaction from them. For example, your goal might be to complete a 10K road race in a specific time—that's a performance goal. On the other hand, "finishing in the top fifty of a 10K road race" is an outcome goal, and there are too many outside factors beyond your control that can affect the outcome.

Make your goals realistic. If you create goals that can't be attained, you're setting yourself up for failure. Dooming yourself to defeat goes against the whole purpose of this exercise.

Here are some reasons we often set unattainable goals:

Other people. Parents, the media, and society often have their own expectations for us. Your goals should be about what you want to attain, not what others expect of you.

Insufficient information. If you don't clearly understand what you are trying to achieve, or you don't know what skills you'll need to master to get there, then it's hard to be realistic.

Demanding your best performance all the time. If you set goals based on your best performance, then you're targeting something that may be too hard to attain consistently. It's better to set goals that raise your average performance.

Don't be too easy on yourself. Some people set their goals too low, whether it's because they're afraid of failing, or because they think that low goals are easier to attain. If that's part of your personality, look for ways to challenge yourself. Do you usually add one new client every quarter? Then go one step further and make your goal to add two or three. Expect great things from yourself.

Be relevant. Goals should help you attain a specific aim. Look out for goals that are just going to keep you busy but are not appropriate to the overall success of your business. If you don't believe that your goals are worthwhile, you won't make the necessary effort to achieve them.

Thinking a Goal Through

When you are thinking about how to achieve goals, ask yourself the following questions to help you focus on the tactics and subgoals you need to accomplish them:

▶ What skills do I need?

▶ What information and knowledge do I need?

▶ What help, assistance, or collaboration do I need?

▶ What resources do I need?

▶ What can block progress?

▶ Am I making any assumptions?

▶ Is there a better way of doing things?

A Goal-Setting Success Story

Edward and Robin made goal-setting an important part of their lives. Edward had been running his own marketing communications firm from his home for over six years, but had only sporadically used goal-setting as a business tool. His wife, Robin, a freelance video producer, was more conscientious in goal-setting, but she too had let it slip. In fact, it took the birth of their first child to make them reevaluate their priorities and sit down and create lists of personal, business, and family goals.

"I was never much of a goal-setter," said Edward, "and I came up with various reasons not to sit down and do this with Robin. We finally got a baby-sitter, armed ourselves with legal pads and pens, and went out to a local coffeehouse for several hours. When we got there, we started talking about what we wanted to accomplish from our respective businesses and what we wanted to do with our lives together. We spent some time visualizing, then started to write down specific goals. For instance, I had recently changed the focus of my business, and I wanted to bring in more clients and improve my income, so I set specific, measurable goals in this area. Robin, on the other hand, needed to rewrite a script she had been working on and show it to certain producers who had expressed interest, and her goals reflected that. We also set some goals together regarding our family, our living situation, our diet, and so forth.

"Once we had the goals written down, we put them in a folder so we could examine them regularly. Now here's the amazing thing: we reached most of our goals. My client list expanded as I intended, as did my income; Robin completed her script on time; we moved into a larger apartment, which was family goal number one. I'm not saying that the goal-setting had made these things happen, but it really felt good to us knowing that we had accomplished what we had set out to do. By writing our goals down, we made them realistic. And because we had done our individual business goals together, we had someone else who knew what we each wanted to accomplish and who could share our success.

"We now have made goal-setting an integral part of our life together. Some time every January, we sit down and do this exercise. It gives us a clearer vision for our future, and it gives us a path toward getting there."

Acknowledging Your Accomplishments

When you work in a home office, you are responsible for giving yourself credit for what you've accomplished. It's much easier to figure out what you haven't done—what projects loom ahead, what sales haven't closed yet, what deadlines still need to be met. In fact, most of us tend to do this. But if one thing should be clear after reading the goal-setting section, it is how important it is for us to acknowledge what we have attained.

Doing this won't be easy, because you'll probably have to break some old, ingrained habits. Try these techniques to make small changes in the way you treat yourself.

Review your accomplishments every day. Before you get up from your desk, spend a few minutes to see what you've achieved. It could be something that seems small or trivial—perhaps reaching someone you've been meaning to call for weeks. Or it could be something important, such as inking a new client. Either way, take the time to give yourself a pat on the back.

Look at your work in progress. The slow-and-steady gains you make along the way to completing some important work will be much more common than explosive finishes. Give yourself some credit for doing this work. It might even help to use a project manager of some sort, so you can see more clearly all the little gains you make on the way to something big.

Share your accomplishments. If you're proud of yourself for having done something well, tell your spouse, a close friend, a relative, or a colleague. It's okay to brag a bit on occasion, if for no other reason than to let people close to you know how satisfied you are about what you've done. If this kind of sharing doesn't come naturally to you, force yourself to call someone and talk about what you've done, even if you only modestly weave it into the conversation.

Reward yourself. You probably send greeting cards, congratulation letters, flowers, or little gifts to others, but when was the last time you did something nice for yourself? It doesn't have to be a new car or a trip — maybe it's that book you've been meaning to read, or that concert you wanted to get tickets for, or that restaurant you wanted to try. In other words, do unto yourself as you would do unto others.

Give Yourself the Tools to Get the Job Done

Ever try to hammer a nail with a screwdriver? Then you know that you need the right tool for the right job. But I've found that many home-based workers handicap themselves by using the wrong tools or by not taking the time to learn how to properly use the tools they have. This can leave them frustrated, negative, and discouraged. On the other hand, the right tools not only get the job done, but they're often fun to use, enlightening, and powerful.

Technology

Think of technology as your tireless business partner. It's probably what made your home office possible in the first place. Beepers, laptops, cell phones, faxes, and e-mail can all increase your productivity. On the other hand, you may also find technology overwhelming. That's why it's necessary to pick and choose so that you find the systems that not only support what you're doing but also help you reach your goals.

For example, a publicist might require word processing software to write press releases, a database manager to track publicity outlets, a fax machine and e-mail account to zap out news announcements; an alphanumeric pager and cell phone for twenty-four-hour press access, a laptop to take on press junkets, and so forth. A massage therapist, on the other hand, might only need a beeper so that he or she can be reached while traveling from client to client. If you are a telecommuter, I urge you to ask management for the tools you need to be more productive. You may have to build a business case for why you need them, but management relies on you to let them know what is needed in a home office. Although it is preferable to have your employer pay for the technology you need to run your home office more efficiently, it is sometimes worth a personal investment in an item that management won't cover, especially if it will dramatically improve the quality of your home office life.

Education and Training

A good boss encourages his or her staff to take classes and seminars to update and hone their business skills. If you telecommute for a larger company, your employer may pay for these classes or may have some kind of tuition reimbursement program. If you're a home-based entrepreneur, you may be able to deduct from your taxes the cost of professional seminars or classes for improving the knowledge or skills you need to operate better in your current job.

Here are some places you can go to improve your skills:

▶ *Trade and professional associations* often offer continuing or professional educational services through their national and local chapters. They also sponsor one-shot seminars where you can both learn and network.

▶ *Local colleges* and universities sponsor continuing education programs where you can brush up on or learn basic business skills— look for classes on computers, accounting/bookkeeping, marketing, management, taxes, and so on. Check out community colleges and area vocational schools as well.

▶ *Computer user groups* are an excellent place to learn ways to take advantage of hardware, software, and communications technologies. Their classes are often taught by members, many of whom are professionals who understand what you need to get out of your system. To find a user group in your area, call the Association of Personal Computer User Groups' locater service at 914-876-6678.

▶ *Trade magazines* and local business journals list seminars and classes. Look at the "calendar" section.

▶ *The Internet* is a growing educational force, and several educational companies that hold online classes have sprung up. This way, you don't even have to leave your home to go to school.

Information

Information is the most vital competitive tool you can use in today's economy. For this reason, devote at least thirty minutes or an hour each day to reading newspapers, trade magazines, newsletters, and other materials that will help you learn more about the issues affecting your business. It's extremely important to stay abreast of new developments as they occur, because that can make or break your ability to compete with larger companies. Find the time to do this: read the *Wall Street Journal* in the morning with your coffee; flip through some industry journals while you're on hold; look at your reading file while you watch TV. One minor caveat: Do not turn your desk into a library by cluttering it up with books and magazines that you read for pleasure—these have no place in your office and can become a major distraction.

The good news is that technology is making it much easier for you to get the information you need. Various Internet services—such as PointCast and Newstracker—will summarize news developments on certain subjects. Some services even forward the information directly to your e-mail box. This way, you don't have to spend time flipping through pages of information that doesn't concern you; you get right to the meat of what has a specific impact on your business.

I would also encourage you to read business books. There's no substitute for learning from experts. And I've found that when I don't have time to read these books, I listen to them. You'll find many top business best-sellers available on tape.

Support Staff

If you've been accustomed to working in a corporate environment, then you know the benefits of a strong support staff. This support staff is just as important in a home office. In chapter 5, Time Management, I get into more detail about delegating, but in general I am in favor of delegating to support staff whenever possible. If you are a telecommuter and your company doesn't have a budget for support staff, look into getting an intern from a local college to help you. Many students are eager to get work experience, and you may be able to get them to help you one afternoon or day a week for free in exchange for learning about your company and your line of work. Entrepreneurs can also hire interns and should bring in support staff whenever possible.

If you cannot get help with your professional responsibilities, at least get help with the chores you have in your personal life. The money you spend will come back to you tenfold in increased productivity and reduced stress.

Know When You Need Help

One of the toughest things about being your own boss is that you don't have many places to turn for help. There are some times when you just don't have the answers and you don't know where to go to get them. It's not always possible to master every skill you need, and when that's the case, it's good to have a support structure around you where you can go to ask for assistance. Who would some of these people be?

- *Professional colleagues.* It's okay to talk with other people involved in your industry, and chances are that you can learn a lot from them, especially when it comes to resources or professional referrals. You can meet your peers at industry association meetings, trade shows, or other professional venues.

- *Mentors.* A common trait among successful individuals is their willingness to share their knowledge and insight. Find someone whose career track you admire, and ask to be taken under his or her wing; you may be surprised at how eager the person is to have you as a protégé.

▶ *Professional Advisers.* Your accountant, attorney, or another professional may have the answers you need. Cultivate relationships with these advisers so that you can take advantage of the depth and breadth of their knowledge.

Watch Out for Naysayers

Earlier in this chapter, I talked about how people often talk to themselves in negative terms. Even more toxic to people who work on their own are the naysayers—people who tell you that you won't accomplish what you set out to do. Consider them your nemesis, because their negative comments can have a profound affect on your well-being and confidence. These are not the people you want to be in your support circle.

I have several methods to help you deal with naysayers: First, you should anticipate it happening. If you expect to encounter naysayers periodically, then their comments won't do as much damage. Second, look for advice only from people you want to emulate, and don't listen to anybody else. Third, don't share your ideas with people who regularly shoot you down; it's just not worth the effort to build yourself back up again.

Have a Support Program

If you find that you're being too hard on yourself, that you're making mistakes, that you're having problems that affect the quality of your work . . . you might want to consider seeking outside help. There's nothing wrong with pursuing therapy. It doesn't mean that there is something wrong with you, and it doesn't make you any less of a success. In fact, success can demand a lot from you, and it's often a good idea to have an impartial party with whom you can openly discuss your hopes, fears, and other issues. You'll find you may gain important perspective on your life, your work habits, and your personal habits.

The most reliable way to find a therapist is to ask someone you know for a referral. But that's not always possible, or you may be a bit embarrassed to ask. If that's the case, you can look under "Psychologists" or "Social Workers" in your Yellow Pages for a counseling referral service, or under "Community Resources" in the front of your White Pages.

PART TWO

Managing Time and Workload

1.) Open Sundry Mail At your desk

Time Management 5

Working at home puts you in one of those good news/bad news situations. The good news is that you get to manage your own time. The bad news is that you *have to* manage your own time! Poor time management is the Achilles heel of many home office workers, because there's nobody else around to help you organize and prioritize. You may yourself be under ongoing deadline pressure, which can lead to overwork, burnout, and other stress-related maladies. In this chapter you will discover the most common and insidious time-eaters and learn tactics that will give you control of your time and help you get more hours out of the day. You'll learn ways to organize your office and your life, and keep them that way. I also give some tips about delegating responsibility, a chief tactic for keeping you from wasting time on things you don't need to be doing.

How Much Time *Do* You Have?

Before we get more deeply into time bandits and how to stop them, let's take a look at how you actually spend your time now. The reason for this exercise is simple—there are only twenty four hours in a day, and as a friend of mine once said to me, You can't make time, so you have to be realistic about what can be accomplished within your given parameters. Managing your time is really a matter of determining what you can squeeze into the day. The first step toward doing this is to figure out how you are currently spending your time.

1. Take a piece of paper (or two or three) and write down estimates of how much time you spend daily on everything you do that does not include work. List the number of hours you spend sleeping, eating, preparing food, being with children and family members, visiting friends in person or talking on the telephone, reading the newspaper, grooming yourself (shaving, showers, makeup, dressing), working out, caring for pets, doing home chores (cleaning up after meals, doing housework, mowing the lawn) and any other personal or maintenance tasks that make up your typical day.

2. Add up all these hours and multiply by seven. Next, include averaged times for tasks you do less frequently, such as food or clothes shopping, attending church, or getting haircuts.

3. Subtract this weekly total from 168 (the number of hours in a week). This will give you the total amount of time you have left over to work.

4. Measure this figure against the amount of time you need to spend working. This will help you to determine if you have a discrepancy.

5. If there are activities missing from your weekly list that you wish you had time for, write these down and save the paper—soon you'll be scheduling time for doing more of what you *want* to do.

Once you've determined how much time you've got to work with, you might want to take a look at how you're spending your time at work. Over the course of a week or so, track how you spend your office time. You don't need to have a formal flow chart. Instead, keep a watch and legal pad handy. Mark the time you start a task and the time you finish. This will help you determine how much time you actually spend doing productive and nonproductive tasks, and you'll learn what places you can manage your time better. For example, you might find that a phone call you think took only five minutes expanded to half an hour because of nonproductive chit-chat. Or perhaps you'll find yourself spending five minutes here or ten minutes there looking for files or reports—little bits of time that add up to hours over the course of a week.

Get Five Hours a Week Free . . . By Being Organized

Organization is your #1 time management tool, just as disorganization is your biggest time-waster. Pawing through the papers on your desk, your computer, or your file cabinet to find the information you need is, without a doubt, one of the biggest time-wasters of all. If you're like most people, you waste about five hours a week at this frustrating and unproductive exercise.

But before you get carried away thinking of all you could do with that extra five hours, carve out just one half-hour today to start sorting. Even if you can only spend a half-hour at a time at this project, you will have a clear desk surface—and a more organized office—in just a few days.

The Way to an Organized Desk

Get a large trash bag and a good-size wastepaper basket. Start sorting, looking at every single paper. You'll be surprised at how much actual trash in the form of unneeded paper you find lurking all over your desk. In fact, about half of what you find there will go directly into the trash or recycling bin.

Professional organizer Ilise Benun suggests that you ask these simple questions as you sort through the paper piles:

- *Do I need this?* If the answer is no, toss it out immediately.

- *Why do I need this?* Be honest. If there's no compelling reason, it goes into the trash.

- *When will I need it?* Again, if you don't know when you'll need it, chances are you won't ever need it. If that's the case, toss it out.

- *What's next for this item?* This will help you determine where to file the item.

▶ *Where would I look for it?* This is *not* Where should I put it? If you think in terms of where you would look for it, it will be easier to find it in the future.

Don't allow yourself to be interrupted during this sorting process. And don't stop for anything—don't settle back and reminisce, don't dart up to return a phone message you suddenly discover amid the rubble, don't fax the clippings you promised but buried under the incoming mail.

There will be time to do these things, but now is the time to throw things away and file items for which you've already got a folder. Make a distribution pile for items to be given or returned to someone else, such as reports or papers for clients or associates, a book or magazine you borrowed, or anything you don't need or want anymore that could be of interest to someone else.

When you've completed all of the above steps, you will have three very useful things: a clean desk, a list of things you need to do, and a clear sense of purpose. Set up the new files, prioritize the items on your list, and take out the trash.

Creating a "Safe" Trash Can

If you're the kind of person who feels uneasy about throwing things away, use a "safe" trash can. Toss papers you aren't sure about into a large trash can. This will be your safe trash. Empty this can every few weeks, giving yourself a grace period so that if you decide you still need something, you can retrieve it. And if you never think about the item again, it goes out at the end of the trash cycle. If you live with other people or have someone who cleans your home office, be sure to ask them not to empty your trash can without checking with you first. Also, keep in mind that you may be digging through this trash can regularly, so throw *only* paper in it. Avoid tossing in banana peels, soda cans, old ham sandwiches, or anything else you wouldn't want to have to see again.

Organize Your Files Efficiently

Filing things away is one thing, but you won't be using your time effectively if you can't find anything in your cabinets. Use these tips to cut down on this time-waster:

Clean regularly. Sort through your file cabinets at least once a quarter and pitch things you no longer need.

Rename your files. Create file names based on the first word that comes to your mind when you create the file. Chances are, if this word comes to you when you are filing it, it will occur to you when you are looking for it.

Create subfolders in each hanging folder. This will also increase the ease with which you can locate things.

Group related hanging files together. Keep client folders in one drawer or part of a drawer, articles you save in another, and so on. Keep your personal files in a drawer separate from all business material.

Have sufficient filing space. Organization is only feasible if you have enough space in your file cabinets. Invest in high-quality, large file cabinets that provide enough space for the material you need to store. The same applies to numbers of files. Some clients or projects merit three or more hanging folders. Sufficient space will make it easier to locate items when you need them.

Use colors. To make files easier to locate, use color-coded files or label your files using different colored pens. For example, use red for hanging and blue for folders that live inside the hanging folders.

Keeping Yourself Organized

Now that you've created an organized and neat work area, your challenge will be to keep it that way. If you let your desk gradually disappear under paperwork, you've lost the time management advantage that you gained by cleaning it up in the first place. Now is the time to acquire the habits necessary to keep yourself on the straight and narrow.

Lists

If you are not a list maker, become one. It will do a lot for your organization, peace of mind, and dependability. Lists keep things from falling through the cracks, and once you've written down a task, your mind is free to concentrate on more important things. Lists also provide a sense of accomplishment, because it feels great to cross an item off your list after you've completed a task.

Be careful not to fall into the trap of creating multiple to-do lists. A single list that acts as a roster of your unfinished tasks is all you need. You want to get away from those messy scraps of paper, sticky notes you post but never look at, or jottings on old gas bill envelopes that you misplace.

A list can be created on paper or computer. I am partial to a computer list because it can be indefinitely added to and subtracted from without creating a mess. I can cut and paste phone numbers to it from my database, and I always know where it is. A computer list also saves me from having to copy phone numbers and addresses generated for my to-do list back into my computer. On the other hand, many people swear by paper lists. My recommendation is to keep as much on computer as possible because it is a tidier way of working. However, if having to create a list on computer will discourage you from creating a list at all, use paper.

Periodically update your to-do list by deleting items. If you are working with paper, do this carefully to make sure you don't overlook an unfinished task and cross off items when you complete them. When I kept paper lists, I did not throw them away immediately after consolidating. The reason: I often found myself needing phone numbers, addresses, and other nuggets of information that I had jotted down on the list but hadn't transcribed.

Schedules (or Freedom through Planning)

Now that you're writing down every task you need to complete, hone your list-making skills by combing through your calendar. Take it out and open it up on your nice clean desk, or open your calendar software, and enter all the deadlines you have coming up. Try not to worry that you will lose freedom by scheduling everything, you will soon see how living with schedules actually creates more free time.

For each task or deadline on your list, analyze the work that needs to be done and break it down by job. Schedule the time needed to complete each job right on your calendar. For example, you might have written *Deadline: May 2, Murray Company presentation.* In the time leading up to that date, pencil in the days on which you will write the proposal, create the budget, meet with your associates and coordinate their presentations, prepare visual aids, and so on until every last detail required for the Murray presentation is blocked out on your calendar. These will be the same items as on your to-do list. Now, even if you're under a tight deadline, you know exactly what you must do and when you will do it. If you need to work evenings or weekends, you've planned for them. Once you've done this, the Murray presentation doesn't look quite so scary, because you know you have time set aside to complete it.

Make a Reading File

Create a single file that contains all the articles from magazines, newspapers, and trade journals you've been meaning to read but never seem to get to. This will do great things for your desktop control. First, it will clear out all the piles of periodicals you've got lying around. Second, it will stop you from feeling guilty about never catching up on your professional reading. The truth is, most of the information in your reading pile is probably out of date by now and even more of it isn't really vital to you anyway. Recycle newspapers that are more than two days old, weekly periodicals that are two weeks old, and monthly journals that are more than two months past their prime.

When you receive new material, quickly skim the table of contents and tear out or clip any articles that seem interesting or pertinent. Put these in a manila file folder marked READING, and then take it along on business trips, to doctors' appointments, to wait for your daughter's ballgame to end—whenever you expect some downtime. After you've read each piece, file it or toss it. Set aside some time every few months to scavenge this file. If Thanksgiving is creeping up, and you still haven't read the articles you put away last spring, toss them.

Keeping a reading file accomplishes two things: it removes reading from your line of vision and organizes it so that you are more likely to take it along with you and actually get it read. Part of learning to manage your reading is managing your expectations of your reading. For example, my husband used to read the *New York Times,* the *Wall Street Journal,* the

Economist, the *Harvard Business Review, Ad Age,* and three monthly trade magazines and assorted other publications. He was incredibly well-read but had no time for anything else. I convinced him to cut back on some reading, and now he frequently remarks that he doesn't feel any less informed than he used to be.

Manage Meetings

Part of being organized is sticking to the time that you have alloted for a particular task, and this includes meetings. With some exceptions, I like to end meetings on time. Unless you are vigilant about sticking to your schedule, meetings can drag on and on—often without a lot of added benefit for the extra time spent. Obviously, meetings must sometimes be extended, but if you make an attempt to start and end meetings on time, you will find yourself better able to manage all of the items on your to-do list.

Put Voice Mail to Work for You

Use voice mail to manage time and cut down on interruptions by making each message work for you. Think of a voice mail message as a tool of your business, and ask yourself if you are using the tool each time you leave someone a message. Using the tool means communicating as much information as possible in your message. Give the person you are calling details of what you need so that he or she can prepare before calling you back. Answer questions so that, whenever possible, your call does not generate a call in return. Of course, you want to avoid being off-putting and appearing that you want to avoid real-time conversations. You can accomplish this by encouraging people to call you with any questions and letting them know when you are reachable.

Have a Place for Everything   OPEN MAil at desk

To keep creeping paper piles from reinfesting your desktop, and to keep yourself from slipping into the situation where your desk controls you, make it a practice to deal with paper as soon as you get it. If it requires action, write the task on your list. If it's something you'll refer to again, file it. If you want to read it later, put it in your reading file. If it's of no particular use or interest, throw it away. The point is to act on it, put it away or throw it away before it takes on a life of its own atop your desk.

Organize Your Computer Files, Too

While you're doing your organization exercises, you also might want to look for ways to organize your computer files more efficiently.

▶ Transfer old or seldom-used files to floppy disks or data cartridges—this frees up disk space and increases your computer's file-retrieval speed.

▶ Create subdirectories on your hard drive so that all related files are saved together in a group.

▶ Give files sensible names so that you can easily identify them without having to open them.

If you think you could be doing a better job of time management, you're not alone. Thirty years ago, there were fewer than a dozen books on the subject. Today, more than a hundred books—plus software, calendars, planners, and hundreds of articles—jostle for more of our time so that they can advise us on how better to manage it!

Control Interruptions

Interruptions are also big time-eaters. Protecting yourself from interruptions means that you are controlling your own schedule. Here are some of the worst culprits and some tactics for keeping them from making off with your time.

The Telephone

Talking on the telephone can rob huge chunks of time from your day. If you jump to answer the phone every time it rings, you'll wonder where the day went.

Stop answering the telephone every time it rings. Set a certain time during the day for collecting your messages and returning phone calls.

Caller ID, available from most phone companies, enables you to know who is calling you so that you can avoid picking up the phone unless you see the phone number of a person whose call you are awaiting.

If you are particularly prone to the tempting, but ultimately time-eating habit of chatting on the phone during the day, try this: Get an egg timer (the quiet kind with sand in it). When you make a call that shouldn't require much of your time, flip the hourglass over and make sure you keep the conversation within your self-imposed limits. Phones that time your calls are also available and will serve as a constant reminder of the amount of time you spend chatting.

Know what you want to accomplish from each phone call, and take notes during all calls to avoid having to spend time clarifying or calling back to check facts. If you have to make a call to a notorious gabber—we all know a few—let the person know at the top of the call that you only have a few minutes to speak.

Let people know when they do not need to return your call so that you don't waste time on unnecessary calls. For example, if you leave someone a message with details of an upcoming meeting, ask that you be called back only if he or she cannot make it. Make sure your message is clear by stating at the end of your message, "If I don't hear from you, I will look forward to seeing you at . . ."

The Fax Machine

Faxes are rarely emergencies. Let them sit, just as the telephone messages do. If you jump up to grab every fax as it scrolls from your machine, you will get off schedule and break your concentration on the task at hand. Go through your faxes and read them all at the end of the day.

When you need to send faxes, do it after regular business hours if possible. This will save you the time of redialing and trying to get past a busy signal. It also keeps similar tasks grouped together so that you can stay on your schedule and focus on your tasks.

Assistants

If an employee interrupts you frequently, he's not saving you time. Make sure that your assistants are truly working in a way that helps you control time. You don't have to make yourself available at a moment's notice. Good time managers are likely to tell employees that they don't have time to figure out solutions for them. They lay out expectations up front and then encourage people to determine the best strategy for meeting these expectations.

My system with my assistants is to have a computer disk for each of them, on which I put a list of tasks. They review the disk's task file when they get into the office. If they have questions, they ask me, but otherwise they leave updates on tasks on the same disk (in boldface type) so that I can review it when it is convenient for me. This system means that I have a record of all requests and answers to my questions and that I don't have to be interrupted.

Errands

A surefire way to cut down on errands is to evaluate every task and determine if you can handle it over the phone rather than going in person. Most items can be purchased over the phone and delivered to you. Even if you have to pay a delivery charge, you will most likely save money as long as the charge is less than the cost of your time to run the errand. A few of the items I have delivered are groceries, shampoo, batteries, stamps, vitamins, moisturizer and other beauty aids, books, computer equipment, and supplies.

> **E**ven if you save just two hours a week with your new time management skills, imagine what you could do with that time. You could, for example, see a movie every week. Or, if you prefer, think of it this way:
>
> 2 hours/week × 52 weeks/year = 104 hours, or a very nice four-day weekend!

Beat Procrastination

Procrastination is an enormous void into which countless hours of valuable time are sucked and never heard from again.

If you can overcome your procrastination habit, you've just bought yourself hours of time each month—maybe a week or two of time every year—depending on the size of your habit. Are you much of a procrastinator? For some of us, it's an ingrained habit, like fingernail biting or leaving the cap off the toothpaste. Of course, the fine art of putting off until tomorrow what you should do today requires much more practice and effort than those other bad habits. And a few nibbled nails don't waste as much of your time—or cost you as much money—as procrastination does.

Here are ten things you can do to help you kick the procrastination habit.

1. Figure out why you're dragging your feet. Sometimes an irrational fear—one we're barely conscious of—is holding us back. Are you afraid that you won't do the job perfectly? Or that you might even fail at it? Maybe it's success that's scaring you. Spend some quiet time to figure this out, and then write these thoughts down so that you can ponder their irrationality.

2. Break the project into small, easy-to-manage tasks. This will make the job seem less oppressive, less vaguely threatening.

3. What if? Ask yourself what's the worst that could happen if you don't do this job. Then ask what's the best thing that could happen if you get it done. This compare-and-contrast exercise can be a great way to motivate yourself.

4. Assign yourself the job. If you let others know that you intend to do it, you're on for the job. Tell at least one other person whose good opinion you value about this project. This makes you accountable. Don't underestimate the power of potential embarrassment to move you to action.

5. Start anywhere. Tell yourself that you only need to write a really bad first draft of the letter. Jot a couple of notes that you intend to use during the phone call. Set up a meeting that will get the process rolling. Action is the key here because one thing really does lead to another.

6. Set a deadline. Creating a deadline will give you a sense of urgency, even if it's artificial.

7. Catch yourself in the act. Be conscious of when you're busying yourself with some other occupation that is nothing more than a stalling tactic. Raising these avoidance mechanisms to the conscious level will help get you back on track.

8. Get it over with. Get started with the project early in the day even if you're not a morning person. Think how much better you'll feel by noon if you've got some, most—or even all—of your loathsome project taken care of!

9. Use treats and shocks. It works for hamsters and it can work for you, too. If you know you'll get the treat of being able to sit down and read your novel for an hour, or call your best friend in the middle of the day, or eat a slice of chocolate cake, you'll be scurrying around that cage to get your work done. On the other hand, if you do procrastinate, you'll be "shocked" by the feeling that you let yourself down, and you'll suffer the deprivation of missing out on your special treat.

10. Make it interesting. If you've been putting off the job because it's plain old boring, find a way to add some zest to it. Can you break the land-speed record for reading a contract? Maybe you can make it the most interesting budget document anyone has ever read. Whatever is facing you, add some challenge to an otherwise dull task.

Delegating

Delegating tasks that can be done more quickly, efficiently, or cheaply by someone else is a very smart time management technique. Are you taking full advantage of it? To answer this question, get out the lists you made earlier in the chapter. The first list shows you exactly what you do with your time; the second, what you need to do; and the third, what you like to do and wish you could do more of.

Look at your first list. Examine it for tasks that could be done just as well by someone else, with or without a little training. Next, look at the first inventory you made of how you spend your nonwork time. Which items from that list can you hire someone to take care of? Shopping? Errands? Dropping off or picking up children?

Figure out what you can reasonably expect to delegate, and calculate how many hours you're likely to save per week. How will you choose to spend that time? If selling is what you do best, but you spend 25 percent of your time on administration and only 12 percent on selling, maybe you can flip those numbers. Perhaps you long to design and implement a whole new marketing plan but until now never seemed to have the time. With this new delegation system, you will soon be well on your way to one.

Remember that just because you *can* do everything yourself doesn't mean that you should. Hiring a service to help with domestic chores, or delegating administrative work to an assistant, frees you to concentrate on the things you do best and enjoy most. Any task you don't like, or one that takes up time better spent on something else, is fair game. The trick is to find a good person to do the job and train him or her well.

> **G**ood time managers are explicit in their instructions and communications. They do not want to discuss or explain things five times, so they do it carefully the first time, making sure that their instructions, requests, and communications are clear. This requires a little more time up front, but is more efficient in the long run.

Some Common Excuses for Not Delegating

For premium efficiency, you should actually delegate as much work as you possibly can. But there's enough of the old-fashioned work ethic in many of us to make it hard to justify farming work out to others. Here are some of the most frequent reasons why people sometimes have trouble letting go.

Money. You may feel that you should do everything yourself so you can hold on to your money. But this kind of thinking keeps many people treading water in their businesses instead of moving ahead. As soon as you begin using the time you've just bought yourself to find more business, you'll make more money. Besides, if you make more money per hour than it costs you to pay someone to clean your house, it doesn't make economic sense to do it yourself. When you hire help, you're making an investment in the future of your business. *Idea:* If you're really concerned about the expense of hiring a part-time assistant, pool resources with a colleague and share the assistant's time as well as the costs.

Time. Another reason people give for not assigning tasks to someone else is that they can't spare the time to do the training. This is often a rationalization for a deeper concern—perhaps a fear of giving up control. If this sounds familiar, write down all your tasks and estimate how long it would take to teach someone to take care of them for you. Then choose one or two jobs that are the easiest to teach and start with them. This will gradually get you used to letting go of minor or routine responsibilities.

Quality. Many people believe that they must do everything themselves because no one else can do it right. And this may actually be true—but it's not a reason to avoid delegating. In fact, a new hire may not do a job as well as you do, especially at first—but look further down the line at the kind of job your assistant can do for you once he or she is trained. People learn to do jobs well, just as you learned—and are still learning—to do yours skillfully and efficiently.

Tasks You Can Delegate

Here are sample lists of tasks you may want to consider delegating or hiring someone to do for you:

OFFICE HELP

File

Organize supplies and storage areas

Answer phones and field routine questions and requests

Update your mailing list and other data entry tasks

Run errands/act as courier

Research

Proofread

Clip relevant articles and create reading file

Open and sort mail

Send out large mailings

Order office supplies

Make routine calls

Obtain business licenses and other official papers

DOMESTIC HELP	Do laundry
	Shop for groceries
	Clean house
	Deliver meals
	Do house repairs and maintenance
	Mow lawn
	Walk dog
	Run general errands
	Plan parties
	Make travel arrangements

Of course, you should be delegating more than just clerical tasks. By hiring a professional to do larger tasks, you not only save time, but you improve the quality of the work that gets done. You use your talents while the people you hire use theirs. Here are a few places to try this:

Writing. Doing this effectively requires a special talent. Think how much more efficient and effective you'd be if you hired a pro to write your press releases or brochure copy.

To find the people you need, look in the Yellow Pages or your local newspaper. Dancers, singers, and other artists are often looking for dependable sources of cash and can make great assistants, so consider putting an ad in a local arts publication or at a dance studio. Look for business cards and ads posted on the message boards in grocery stores and community centers. Probably the best, most reliable method is to get recommendations from friends and colleagues. Do a careful search—don't just hire the first person you talk to. The time spent up front will pay off in the long run.

Handling payroll. Many services will do everything from figuring out taxes and social security payments to cutting the checks and deducting the amounts from your bank account. Think how long it would take you to do all these steps.

Bookkeeping. If you're not a financial wizard, or if you're simply too bored or too busy to keep your own books, you'd be smart to let someone skilled (and interested) take care of this painstaking chore.

Estimating and paying quarterly taxes. Or doing any number of higher-level accounting procedures. Again, this can be a difficult and tedious chore. Leaving it to the experts will ensure that it gets done right while you are taking care of something you have the talent or skill for.

E-mail—Getting and Sending It Efficiently

I first started using e-mail as a way of saving time and making myself more efficient. But over the years, I've watched this time-saver become a time-waster.

Once, not so long ago, e-mail was a novelty. It was fun to get, fun to send, and usually got the attention of the recipient quickly. Now it's a different story. E-mail is everywhere—just think how much time it takes you (and what a chore it seems) to answer the electronic messages you get. And no doubt you regularly find yourself sifting through tons of annoying junk e-mail (also known as "spam"). Here are some tips to help you wade through the messages you get—and make sure the e-mail you send is welcomed and responded to promptly.

▶ Check your e-mail at specific times during the day. You don't need to drop everything whenever you see or hear that a message has landed in your box. Instead, set aside a block of time in the morning, and perhaps another in mid- or late afternoon to scan and respond to your messages.

▶ Not every e-mail really requires a reply. Before you fire back a response, make sure it's necessary. If you feel rude not responding at all, it's fine to send an e-mail saying "Got it, thanks" and no more.

▶ When the subject lines tip you to a "free offer" or any other type of junk e-mail coming your way, delete it. Don't waste your time reading these messages.

▶ Find out if your Internet service provider offers a blocking service, which refuses e-mail that comes from certain addresses used frequently by spammers. You can also keep track of where most of your junk e-mail comes from; then program your e-mail software to automatically send these files to your "trash."

▶ When you send e-mail, be as brief as possible. Make it your personal challenge to say what you mean in as few lines as possible. Be very careful not to send anything longer than one screen.

▶ If you have a lengthy document to transmit, attach it as a separate file. In the cover screen, briefly sketch its contents and note the due date of whatever response is required.

▶ Be careful who's on your "joke" list. Many people find that they're deluged with jokes and various forwarded e-mails that block up their accounts and eat up their time. Show some discrimination when you forward "interesting" e-mails. Jokes should go only to people who you know enjoy receiving them. And whatever you do, don't waste your or anyone else's time with things such as Internet chain letters and bogus virus alerts that show up from time to time.

Overwork 6

F or a home-based worker, the risk of falling into a destructive pattern of overwork is high. You have little chance to compare your work habits with colleagues, and fewer opportunities to use associates as sounding boards. Thus, you can lose your way without ever realizing it. For home-based entrepreneurs, just knowing that the responsibility for the success or failure of your business is all on your shoulders can be a heavy burden. That pressure can push your work habits into overdrive.

This enormous sense of responsibility can lay the groundwork for unhealthy work patterns—and can even create the addiction to work. You begin to thrive on being in control, working nonstop, and being the most important and powerful person in your own world. You get a high out of solving all the problems, making all the decisions, and, above all, being needed.

The term workaholic gets tossed around a lot as humorous exaggeration, but the condition is no joke. Like any other addiction, workaholism is treacherous. You don't realize you're developing a problem until you are deeply in its grip. By then, denial sets in, and it's not easy to admit that there may be something wrong.

In this chapter you'll learn about the symptoms of overwork, take a test to see if you're headed in that direction, and learn how to be highly productive *without* being yoked to your business twenty-four hours a day, seven days a week. You'll also read about some entrepreneurs who've successfully battled the problem of overwork. And you may be surprised to learn how our society sends out the not-so-subtle message that keeping up a grueling work schedule is a desirable, even glamorous, way of life.

Burnout: What Is It and Where Does It Come From?

Burnout is a term that is sometimes used casually to describe anyone who's just had a bad week. But technically, burnout is the consequence of a long pattern of overwork. It is characterized by a profound state of emotional exhaustion, a feeling of being totally drained, of having nothing left inside. In some cases, it is a way of coping with stress that can no longer be endured. In advanced stages of burnout, people withdraw psychologically, detach themselves from the work they're doing, and can suffer physical ailments ranging from headaches to much more serious illnesses.

If you suspect that you may be suffering from burnout, take some comfort from knowing that it mainly strikes those with the highest standards. Dr. Herbert Freudenberger, who coined the term burnout in 1970, says that the condition is "pretty much limited to dynamic, charismatic, goal-oriented men and women."

In his book *Burnout: The High Cost of High Achievement*, Freudenberger points out that a person exhibiting its symptoms may not be a very sympathetic figure. He or she may be angry, cranky, critical, inflexible, and resistant to any assistance, especially suggestions about change. And organizational psychologist, Dr. Cary Cherniss says that the burned-out person is usually the last to realize that he or she is having a problem. That's a tough combination. To get some idea if you could fall into this category, take the quiz below.

Check Yourself with These Questions

How do you know if you're overworking? Put a check mark next to each question to which you answer yes.

- ▶ Are you forgetting things lately (keys, appointments, deadlines)?
- ▶ Do you feel angry and frustrated whenever anyone interrupts your work?
- ▶ If you're less than constantly busy, do you feel bored and at loose ends?
- ▶ Are you less able to laugh at a joke than you used to be?
- ▶ Do you avoid meeting friends (for lunch, tennis, or other social occasions) because you're afraid that you'll miss something critical in the office?
- ▶ Do you have trouble setting priorities and delegating work?
- ▶ Are you drinking or eating more than you should?
- ▶ Do you skip exercise because you feel you're too busy to take time off?
- ▶ Is your refrigerator nearly empty most of the time?
- ▶ Are you having more physical complaints than usual—headaches, stomach problems, lingering colds, trouble sleeping, or trouble waking up?
- ▶ Have you promised yourself that you'd delegate more, then failed to do so?
- ▶ Do you begin each day with an ambitious to-do list and wind up feeling frustrated because so many items are left undone at day's end?
- ▶ Have friends or family told you lately that you don't "seem like yourself"?
- ▶ Have you lost or gained more than five pounds over the past several months?
- ▶ Do you lack the energy you used to have and feel tired much of the time?
- ▶ Has a family member or close friend told you that he thinks you're working too hard?

▶ Do you carry your cellular telephone whenever you go out?

▶ Is work your chief—or only—source of pleasure in life?

▶ Do you say you'll stop work at a certain time and then ignore your resolution?

▶ Are you working more now but feeling less satisfied with what you've accomplished?

▶ Do you resent people who take time off?

Add up your yes answers and read the evaluation that matches your score below. Although the quiz is informal and unscientific, you should take a high score very seriously and look closely at your work habits.

Your score

1–4 You're leading a fairly balanced life. You can even skip this chapter and come back to it at a later date if you think you need it. You may be working hard to run your business, but you are not afraid to delegate tasks and take breaks from your own work.

5–8 You're under some stress from overwork but probably not in danger of burnout. Although you may occasionally work harder than you should and let your work cut into your personal time, you have enough breaks built into your schedule that you are successfully holding burnout at bay. *Your challenge:* Continue to schedule time off—and take it!

8–11 You are working too hard and flirting with burnout. Look carefully at your work habits to find places you can cut back. You may not be burned out yet, but your lifestyle has you on a path for sure burnout. If you keep up this pace, you may soon find yourself with health problems, conflict in your personal life, and a job that is suffering because you have made careless mistakes.

11–15 You're a serious candidate for burnout and may be in its early stages, which is hampering your work and personal relationships. Chances are that you are experiencing some physical symptoms as a result of the schedule you are keeping. The strong foundation of your personal relationships may be eroding gradually, and you may be making mistakes in your work without realizing it.

15 or more You are most likely dealing with the symptoms of burnout every single day. Your work habits are jeopardizing your physical and emotional health. There's a good chance that you are not able to do your work effectively, and you may need to talk with someone.

What's Wrong with Working Too Much?

Maybe you're on your own with no family obligations and have a brand-new business that you're struggling to launch successfully. Maybe the bottom line is all you see when you close your eyes at night and right now that's fine with you. What's the problem, you may ask, with working all the time? Why shouldn't I give it all I've got? And who's to say I work too much?

Good questions. The first and most obvious reply is that you could be endangering your physical or emotional health and you might even be jeopardizing relationships with people who are important to you.

But there's another reason for trying to keep a balance between your work and personal life that may surprise you. A team of researchers in Sweden found that a group of upper-level managers who worked twelve to fourteen hours a day were not necessarily more productive than those who worked far less. They counted such activities as writing reports, creating budgets, making telephone calls, attending meetings, and so forth as work time and discovered that the most productive executives did actual work only about six and a half hours a day. The rest of the time they spent reflecting, planning, thinking through problems, or even meditating. In jobs that require creativity, imagination, and higher-order thinking, this kind of work pattern may be much more productive.

Edith, Stan, and Harry: Case Histories

Edith, Stan, and Harry don't know each other, but they have a great deal in common. Each gradually fell under the spell of overwork. Neither understood what was happening until symptoms of burnout nearly destroyed their personal lives and threatened to drive them away from the work they liked and the workstyle they had fought for.

Edith couldn't believe that her good idea and hard work had paid off so fast. Just two years after launching a tutoring service for middle-school math and science students, she had two responsible employees and a client list three times larger than the one she had projected in her business plan. Her success had bought her a high-tech home office setup, a dozen laptops for use by her pupils, a new car, and the kind of sophisticated professional wardrobe she used to dream about. But she was also 20 pounds overweight, depressed, not sleeping well, and fighting with her husband on the few occasions they managed to spend time together.

When Edith finally consulted a doctor and revealed her six-day-a-week, 7 A.M. to 10 P.M. work schedule, she learned that she'd become a victim of her own success: "It turned out I'd poured so much of my life into this project that there was nothing left over for my personal life. I was neglecting my husband, my friends, and my physical health, all for the 'good cause' of professional success." It took her several months of struggle to make the necessary changes. "I needed a tutor myself, so I could learn how to balance my life again," she said.

Here are the steps Edith took to ease her overwork:

1. She began keeping a work journal so that she could tell exactly how she was spending her time. She kept track of her specific work activities over the course of several weeks, writing down what she did, when she did it, and how much time it took.

2. She used that journal to decide exactly which tasks did not require her personal attention.

3. She began to delegate more responsibilities to her two capable assistants.

4. She made a firm commitment to cut her work schedule so that she would have at least three evenings a week at home and at least half of every Saturday off.

5. She used some of her newfound time off to begin exercising, which decreased her stress and increased her perspective on work versus her personal life.

Stan was happy when his company announced a telecommuting program. It would mean less commuting time and perhaps a chance to catch up on his work, and he could use the extra time to see his family. Unfortunately, the opposite happened. Losing his administrative help as part of the telecommuting program meant that he had more work on his plate, not less. Being out of the office also generated more e-mail and phone calls for him because everyone who needed to reach him had to do it through technology. Soon his beeper, e-mail, and fax were controlling his life, and he was getting up earlier and earlier each day to get a handle on his work. He didn't want to complain, because he liked the company he worked for and knew that there was steep competition for his job.

Stan finally sought some help. He spoke to management and talked to his peers to find out how they managed the increased workload. Over time, he started to get a handle on his work and cut down on his hours. He took the following steps:

1. He told clients and customers how he wanted to be reached. The beeper was for emergencies, the fax for orders, and phone calls for problem resolution. That helped him prioritize his work and handle important things first. This was a major step in cutting down on his hours.

2. He set realistic goals. Stan realized that he may not be able to keep up with all of the reading he used to do. He read only essential publications and tried to stop worrying about the rest. He opened his mail once every few days instead of every day.

3. He focused. With the help of his manager, Stan focused on what he needed to do to succeed in his job. He focused on making sure that he was taking care of the important responsibilities and staying on top of his area of expertise.

At first, Harry was thrilled to be out of the rat race. At age forty-three, he resigned from a Big Six accounting firm to start his own software company. But after a few months, he found that trading his suit and briefcase for khakis and a sweatshirt didn't really make his life any easier. Being his own boss was even more demanding than struggling to stay ahead in the competitive corporate environment. Instead of working fifty to sixty hours a week, Harry found himself working close to ninety. Instead of taking two weeks' vacation a year, he limited time away to weekends, and he spent most of those chained to his laptop and cell phone. He sold his boat, not because he couldn't afford it, but because he never had time to use it. He yelled at his twin boys whenever they toddled into his office to catch a glimpse of their father. He sent his wife off alone to parties and family gatherings so that he could "catch up" with paperwork.

The trouble was, Harry never caught up, never saw his family, rarely relaxed, and at the end of two years away from the rat race was exhausted and depressed. It was only after he admitted that he was making an unacceptable number of mistakes and errors in judgment in running his business that Harry began to see a counselor about his workaholic tendencies.

Here are the steps Harry took:

1. He made a commitment to see the counselor regularly so that he could talk about his overwork and gain some insight into why it was occurring. He admitted that he had a problem controlling his work habits, and he acknowledged that they were disrupting his life.

2. After months of counseling, he spent two weeks on a small island off the coast of Georgia with his wife and kids, but without his laptop or cell phone.

3. He hired a personal organizer to help him work "smarter not harder."

4. He made a commitment to himself—and to his wife—that he would be "off work" at a reasonable time each night and that he wouldn't work more than two weekends a month.

5. He eventually took on an assistant who helped him stay organized, saving him a significant amount of time.

Symptoms of Overwork

Did you notice that the patterns and symptoms of overwork were similar in all three case studies? Your first step toward overcoming overwork is being able to recognize its effects on you. Here are Dr. Freudenberger's classic symptoms of overwork leading to burnout. They fall into three categories: physical, behavioral, and emotional.

1. Physical Symptoms

Sleeplessness. Getting proper rest is critical to your mental and physical well-being. But many people in the grip of overwork find that they can't turn off their brains at night and fall asleep easily. Or they may finally drop off, only to awaken in a couple of hours with their minds racing, unable to get back to sleep.

Exhaustion. If you are sleeping soundly at night but still feel exhausted, you could be experiencing a symptom of overwork and burnout. It's possible to feel exhausted even if you're *not* having trouble sleeping. Chronic fatigue can be brought about by being in a constant state of tension, worry, or anxiety.

Headaches and back pain. Anyone suffering from chronic headaches or back pain should consult a doctor in order to rule out physical disease. Frequently, headaches are the body's way of alerting us that something is wrong somewhere. The same is true of back pain. Once your doctor has ruled out serious physical problems as an underlying cause, give some thought to the ways in which your lifestyle may be contributing to the pain. Don't keep dosing yourself with over-the-counter painkillers. Take some time to find out exactly what your body is trying to tell you.

Frequent or lingering colds. When you're under a lot of stress, you're more vulnerable to catching the common cold. Getting lots of colds, or having trouble shaking a persistent one, is part of the vicious cycle that starts when you lose sleep, neglect proper nutrition, and fail to get regular exercise.

Chest pains. These can be terrifying because chest pain is one of the symptoms of a heart attack. Immediately check with your physician or go to the emergency room of your local hospital if you have chest pain. But if there is no apparent physical cause for your discomfort, your frightening symptoms could turn out to be the high price you are paying for overwork, stress, and burnout.

2. Emotional Symptoms

Changes in temperament. If you used to have a pretty good sense of humor and were relatively easygoing but lately feel tense, serious, or sad, you could be suffering from overwork and related stress. According to Freudenberger, these manifestations of overwork are frequently misdiagnosed as depression and treated with antidepressants when the real cure might come from a lifestyle change.

Lack of trust. Overwork can cause some people to become less trusting and to feel that they must control everything themselves. They'll read more into a situation than is actually there and will get involved in tasks they should delegate because they no longer think that colleagues or subordinates are capable.

3. Behavioral Symptoms

Withdrawing from friends. Failing to return friends' phone calls, skipping parties or get-togethers, and even failing to send holiday cards (if that has been your custom) can be signals that work has become a substitute for a healthy and satisfying social life.

Impatience and anger. If you find yourself losing your temper more often and more quickly than you used to, take a look at your work patterns. In his studies of people suffering from burnout, Freudenberger found that they were so impatient that they gave instructions quickly and curtly, leaving out important details. Then they became furious when people didn't follow through correctly.

Popular Images Can Be Destructive

How do we let ourselves get into self-destructive work patterns? One possibility is that we're constantly bombarded by messages that glorify overwork. People working nonstop are portrayed in movies, television shows, and even commercials and magazine ads as having attractive and even glamorous lifestyles.

The cellular telephone is a perfect example because it has become a status symbol. It implies that you're very busy and constantly in demand. And talking on the telephone while you drive is no longer the ultimate symbol of your importance—now you're nobody unless you've got a phone glued to your ear while you shop for groceries, hurry down the sidewalk, or wait for the elevator.

All these images have led many contemporary adults to feel as if being less than constantly busy is like not having a date for the prom.

Neglecting good health and hygiene. If you eat lunch at your desk nearly every day and grab dinner on the run, that could be a sign that you're not taking care of your physical well-being. The same is true if you find yourself running out of clean laundry or dressing carelessly to "save time" for more important things—like work.

What to Do If Overwork Is a Problem

Let's say that you've decided that maybe you're working more now and enjoying it less. Possibly, you're even getting less done. Where do you begin to remedy the situation?

There are a number of practical strategies you can try to cut down on the amount of work that claims your time. But before we discuss these, let's first look at how to cope with the very idea of working less.

The first thing to know is that there is no remedy for someone who doesn't want to change. Those who truly have an addiction to work won't be able to envision that they might be doing better by doing less. When overwork has an addictive component, it may be shoring up a precarious sense of self or helping to avoid reality, according to Dr. Cary Cherniss, professor of organizational psychology at Rutgers University. And that makes it especially hard to let go of.

But let's assume that you have bought into the idea that you're working more than is good for your personal well-being or even for the overall health of your business.

The next step is to understand that your life has been structured around work and that you may find it difficult to make the change you'd like. Think of it as withdrawal; the idea is to wean yourself gradually with these five steps.

Step 1 First monitor how much you're working. How many hours a day? How many days a week?

Step 2 Don't try immediately to cut back, say, from fourteen to eight hours a day. Look at how you're spending those hours. Then take just one hour and commit to doing something completely different.

Step 3 Choose an activity that's very different from your job. Make sure it's fun or rewarding in some way. Play a sport, read something pleasurable, do yoga, listen to music, or maybe see an old friend.

Step 4 At first, spend only that one hour away from work a couple of times a week.

Step 5 Make that hour off part of your daily schedule. Gradually add another . . . and then another until you've cut back to a pace that's more in keeping with a healthy and balanced life.

If you believe you're involved in so many projects that you can't cut back on your working hours, take a hard look at every facet of these compulsory commitments:

▶ *Is every item on the list truly that critical?* Let's say that you're due to give a speech. Do you really need to research that topic from the ground up, or could you pull together a good talk from previous notes or give a shorter talk and open it up to a question-and-answer forum? Maybe you'll find that you don't need to reinvent the wheel every time for every commitment.

▶ *Are you the only one who can do it?* If it is critical that something be done, is it absolutely necessary that *you* be the one to do it? You might want to exercise the option of telling people that you're over-committed and recommending an associate or colleague who could handle certain of these projects equally well.

▶ *Is it urgent?* Make sure that you're not holding yourself hostage to dictatorial deadlines. Are you realistic about how pressing your deadlines really are? Does the design for your new logo absolutely have to be done this week? Some deadlines are firm, but a surprising number may turn out to be arbitrary.

▶ *Is technology running your life?* With fax machines, cellular telephones, beepers, and laptop computers, it's easy to get the impression that work is everywhere and must be attended to at every minute. Not so. These high-tech items are there for your convenience. You should be in charge of deciding what's urgent and what merely *seems* urgent because the call came in on your cell phone.

▶ *Are you trying to prove something?* Many telecommuters and entre-preneurs fear that if they don't perform at extremely high levels, they risk being returned to an office or failing at their business venture. Don't be driven by this pressure. Working outside an office envi-ronment has automatically made you more productive because every hour of every day you're coping with many fewer interrup-tions. And just think of all that time you save by not commuting!

Practical Strategies for Streamlining Work

Set priorities. Determine which tasks or issues are most impor-tant to your goal. If you try to keep on top of everything, you run the risk of doing nothing well. Your focus should be a limited number of tasks that are required to make you excel at your job. Create a list of your priorities, and when requests or other items unrelated to those priorities cross your desk, delay working on them until you have handled the priorities.

Be priority driven, not interruption driven. Most business offices are interruption driven. That is, the telephone rings, faxes appear, co-workers come into your office, people call you into meetings, and any number of other interruptions intrude on the work you need to get done. But when you work in a home office, you don't need to be at the mercy of these time-stealers. Take advantage of working at home by putting these practices to work for you:

▶ *Give your home and cellular phone numbers out very selectively.* It's stressful for you to be on-call everywhere you go and at every hour of the day or evening. It's also confusing for people to have a vari-ety of numbers for reaching you. Provide most business associates with only your business line—and then make sure that you are reachable at that number during your designated work hours.

▶ *Avoid answering the phone every time it rings.* As long as you have voice mail, an answering machine, or a secretary, there is no reason to pick up your phone whenever it happens to ring. Have a time of day when you receive calls and let your machine/voice mail/assistant take calls at other times of the day.

▶ *Don't let other people set your priorities for you.* Just because someone sends you an overnight package, a fax, or an e-mail, it doesn't mean that you have to stop what you are doing and respond. Mail doesn't need to be opened more than a few times a week, and most faxes can sit in your machine for days without dire consequences.

▶ *Train people around you not to expect an immediate response from you.* By responding immediately to requests, you set up an expectation that you are always available. Get into the habit of not responding to all e-mail immediately. Practice saying no by using the phrase, "I can't get to that right now, but let me call you Tuesday so we can discuss it."

▶ *Curb the beeps.* Let people know the way you prefer to be contacted. A man in the audience of one of my presentations shared a story about how he cut down on interruptions caused by nonstop beeps from co-workers and customers. His strategy was to create a matrix for reaching him that was organized by type of request. The sheet delineated what kind of problem or request justified beeping him, what requests he wanted to receive via the phone, and when a fax or e-mail would work just as well. Not only did the matrix cut down on interruptions, it also made him more effective in meeting the needs of his associates because he had regained control of his work time.

Create a work schedule and stick to it. Overwork is an occupational hazard for home office workers because we are either in or near the office at all hours of the day and night. Without a physical division between office and home life, work can spread like weeds, invading all the space around us. We can prevent this from happening by setting a time for beginning and ending our days, just as if we still worked in an office. Sometimes we will still need to put in longer hours, but for the most part, we'll have a much better chance at working "normal" hours.

If sticking to strict work hours isn't possible, create some leeway for yourself by limiting the amount of "overtime" you will put in during any given week or month. If you have trouble getting yourself to stop work, try scheduling meetings outside of the office at the end of the day.

When you stop work at the end of the day, close your home office. Turn off the computer, turn down the ringer on your business phone line, and shut off the light at your desk.

When clients or associates call you outside your designated work hours or on weekends, ask if you can get back to them during business hours. Of course, there will be times when you'll need to make exceptions and be flexible. But for the most part, you want to let people know that you are available only at certain hours.

Learn to say no. If you find yourself agreeing to do things that you later wish that you had declined, build in some extra decision time for yourself. When someone calls with a request, tell her you'd like to call her back in a few minutes. This will give you time to think carefully about how you would like to respond. Take that time also to build your resolve about saying no and find a gracious way to say it.

Use goals as gatekeepers. Once you've determined what you are trying to attain, you will have an easier time deciding exactly which projects

Saying No without Being Negative

If the idea of saying no seems harsh to you, think of it as the act of taking care of yourself. Put another way, saying no simply means that you've set limits for yourself and that the request you are declining is outside those limits.

If, for example, someone wants you to take on a job that you'd prefer not to do, you can say "That sounds exactly like something Mary Jones could do for you very well." If pressed, you can explain that you're too busy right now, no longer do that type of work, or whatever other reason you have for turning it down.

You can also say no to certain things by defining what is *within* your limits. Instead of saying "I don't take calls before 9 A.M. or after 6 P.M." you can say that you *are* available nine hours a day, from 9 A.M. until 6 P.M. Always try to turn no into a positive. The key is to offer alternatives, say what you are willing to do, and always be gracious.

you should take on. For instance, if you want to build a corporate clientele, you may need to turn down small jobs that can take time and energy away from going after or properly servicing those larger clients.

If one of your goals is to cut down on time spent working and to take better care of your health or personal relationships, you may have to let an appealing job or choice assignment go to someone else.

Take Back Your Nights

About a year ago, I was slipping into bad habits in my home office: namely, going back to my desk at about 8:30 or 9:00 at night and working until midnight or 1 A.M.

There is nothing wrong with putting in some nighttime hours when you work at home. One of the pleasures of working at home is being able to have a flexible schedule that enables you to work when it suits you.

However, the kind of pattern I had slipped into was not so positive. The dangerous thing was that I was starting to count on the night hours to stay up to date with my work. I was semiproductive during the day but often saved proposal writing and other work for the evening. The downside of this habit was that it gradually trained me to be less productive during my weekdays because I counted on nights or weekends to get loads of work done.

If you find yourself slipping into the same kind of pattern, you need to reclaim your workdays for your own. If you doubt the feasibility of cutting out your nighttime work, keep in mind that you probably finish most of your work before a vacation, a long weekend when you will be out of town, your honeymoon, or before other times that you will not be able to work.

The following steps helped me to take back my private time. I hope that they help you to do the same.

Sketch out your day. Nighttime work is often a result of bad planning. Before you know it, the day has evaporated and you still have important items to complete. Each morning, make a short list of the items you must accomplish that day. Start on those first.

Take control of interruptions. If you let phone calls, staff, or other distractions keep you from completing tasks during the day, you're losing productive hours. You have to control them before they impinge on your work. For example, tell your staff that you are unavailable for the morning, and ask them to save all questions for later in the day. Turn off the ringer on your phone, and return calls every few hours.

Ignore your house. Taking care of errands during the day is fine, but if they have been becoming a larger and larger part of your workday, you need to curtail them. Make a conscious effort to go a few weeks without doing any personal errands or tasks during the day. This will break you of the habit. Once you have learned to handle these chores instead of letting them handle you, you can slowly reintroduce them into your routine.

Start earlier. The problem with working late is that you then sleep late and a vicious cycle is created. I broke it by forcing myself to get up early. Day one was tough, but it gets a little easier each day.

Pull your personal life out of your office. If you keep personal items—for example, your flight reservation for your weekend away, your personal phone numbers, and items you are likely to need in the evening— in your office, you will be lured back to your work area and may start burning the midnight oil. Instead, have a place that is separate from your office for writing thank-you cards, storing personal phone numbers, and keeping other personal items organized.

Put e-mail in its place. E-mail is a great productivity tool, and I rely heavily on it. However, it can also be a time sink if you let it run you. Have one or two times of the day when you check e-mail, rather than logging on every hour to see who is trying to reach you. Answer only essential e-mails during work hours; save social messages for the end of the day when you are winding down.

Check your priorities. If you simply cannot accomplish all your work without regularly working nights and weekends for months on end, you may want to check your focus. Clearly defined goals will enable you to focus on specific items and take extraneous stuff off of your to-do list. I have created an A-list and a B-list. B is for items I want to get to; A is stuff that has to be done soon. *The difference:* B doesn't keep me at my desk at night.

Letting Go of Bad Habits

It can be difficult to let go of bad work habits, especially if you always thought they were good habits exactly *because* you were working so hard. Letting go requires an adjustment of your attitude not only toward work but also toward the world. Here are some things you might want to try.

1. Quit thinking that everyone's life depends on whether or not you stick to your daily schedule and to-do list. Enjoy being just a speck in the universe.

2. Count your commitments, then cut them. Make a list of your work responsibilities, putting the items in order of importance. Now draw a line across the midpoint of the list. Take a hard look at everything that falls below that line. Find at least one thing—preferably two—that can be eliminated completely from the bottom of the list.

3. Stop doing two things at once all the time. It's efficient to flip through the mail while listening to your phone messages, and there's no reason why you can't sort mail into piles while you're on the line with a garrulous client. But some things deserve your complete focus. Make sure that you're not *habitually* performing at least two things at once. It's bad for your nervous system, and it's really not necessary.

4. Find out if you're doing what you mean to do. Write down the number of hours each week you spend doing everything—from eating and sleeping to budgeting and ordering supplies, to talking with your spouse. You may be surprised at how you're spending the bulk of your time. Study the list and make sure it reflects your priorities and goals.

5. Practice patience. Try being as patient with others as you hope they would be with you.

6. Give things the rocking-chair test. When you're sitting in that rocker at age eighty-two, what would you like to gaze back on? Unbroken weeks and months of racing to meetings and dashing off proposals? Or those summer weeks at the lake, fishing and tossing a Frisbee around with your kids?

Stress 7

Stress is the result of most of the factors I've discussed so far in this book, or will discuss in the chapters that follow. Having trouble getting motivated? You'll feel stress. Can't handle setbacks? Stress. Isolation, overwork, and poor time management all breed stress. A poor work environment, a strained relationship, or an inconsistent diet are also stress producers. You get the picture. Unless you're able to control and manage your stress, you will find it nearly impossible to conquer any of the other issues related to working from home.

The corporate world has recently begun to understand the impact of long-term stress on their employees. Many have put in place intervention and stress management programs to make people more productive and happy in all aspects of their work and personal lives. And if you're a corporate telecommuter, you may be able to take advantage of some of these programs. But for the most part, when you work from home, you're on your own to identify where your stress comes from and to look for ways to reduce it. This chapter will help you understand where your stress originates. You'll learn how to keep a stress diary, which can help you to come up with an action plan to remove stress from your life. I've also provided some practical, time-tested techniques for lowering stress levels and some excellent relaxation techniques to help you take it easy.

What Is Stress?

Stress is anything that disturbs your healthy mental or physical well-being. Although stress can help protect us when we face certain physical or emotional events, ongoing stress can also cause serious, negative side effects

Stress comes in two forms—short-term stress and long-term stress. Short-term stress is usually associated with some sort of immediate stimulus that sends a shot of adrenaline into your system. The result is a quick burst of energy that some people describe as the fight-or-flight reaction. You may feel butterflies in your stomach or suddenly burst out in sweat. Although these reactions are not necessarily pleasant, their effects are short-lived, and you may even find them beneficial.

Long-term stress can be more problematic and is often associated with fatigue, drooping morale, and health problems. In the first stage of stress, you may react to a stressful situation with a burst of energy and positive, effective actions. But if this level of stress is sustained over time, these positive feelings may turn into anxiety and frustration, and the quality of your work may begin to suffer. In the third stage of sustained long-term stress, you may start to feel a sense of failure, and your health may begin to suffer. Finally, if high levels of stress continue unabated, you can end up experiencing depression, burnout, a panic attack, or another form of stress-related illness.

Where Stress Comes From

Stress is influenced by a number of factors, both internal and external. Work, of course, can be a significant component. A looming deadline, a demanding client, a vague manager, or a constantly ringing telephone all contribute. When you start to work from home—either as an entrepreneur or as a telecommuter—you'll find that adjusting to your new location and role will be stressful. As a telecommuter, for example, you may suddenly find yourself out of the loop, and this lack of face-to-face communication may breed stress. And if you're an entrepreneur, the constant need to generate income and maintain the health and well-being of your business can create more stress than you can take.

But there are other factors that don't immediately have to do with work. With your office and your home in such close proximity, it's easier for personal and family problems to creep into your work life. Environmental factors, such as noise or your own disorganized clutter, can further compound your work stress. For example, you may find yourself frustrated by a particularly difficult and time-sensitive project, and although you're able to handle that stress, you lose it when the neighbor's gardener shows up with the leaf blower. In other words, multiple stimuli are much harder to handle than single areas of stress.

To help you recognize stress and begin the process of dealing with it, I've put together a short list of stresses you are likely to encounter. There are, of course, many more.

- Too much work
- Fear of having your accomplishments overlooked
- Too little work
- Deadlines and time pressures
- Having to perform beyond your abilities
- Keeping up with new developments
- Demands from customers or clients
- Demands from your boss
- Lack of contact with co-workers
- Lack of information, support, or advice
- Responsibility
- Lack of planning
- Unclear goals
- Having to overcome obstacles
- Disruptions

Working from home also makes it much harder to escape your personal stresses. If you're an entrepreneur, your personal financial obligations are intrinsically linked to your professional performance. Ill-health can keep you out of work, which keeps you from producing income. Even if you enjoy a stable corporate job as a telecommuter, you may now find it more difficult to get away from the factors that cause you stress than you did when you worked outside of the home.

Your Personality

No doubt you've heard about Type A personalities—they often court stress and, at their most extreme, may be addicted to it. Some physicians believe that this situation occurs because stress increases the levels of a neurotransmitter called noradrenaline in our system. This can give a feeling of confidence and elation that Type A people thrive on. If you fall into this category, you may find yourself subconsciously delaying work because you get a rush from deadlines, or you may be creating a particularly stressful environment because you actually enjoy it.

Other aspects of your personality will also have an impact on your stress levels. Perfectionism is a major culprit, because a perfectionist's unattainably high standards can never be satisfied. Neediness is another cause. Some people require the attention of others, and not getting it can lead to dissatisfaction and stress. This is something that telecommuters should be particularly aware of, because they don't always have the support or social structure that exists in a more traditional office.

Survival Stress

When you're put in a threatening situation, you get what experts refer to as survival stress. The threats can be either emotional or physical. Although we tend to think of survival in terms of extreme cases—you're cornered by a wild animal, you see a tractor-trailer bearing down on you, your lover leaves you—we may experience this type of stress for more moderate reasons.

In survival stress, your body is going through physical changes caused by the release of adrenaline. You get the feeling of a sugar rush because the adrenaline is mobilizing your body's sugars to give you added strength and speed. Blood flow to your skin and certain other organs is reduced in order to prevent injury when you are hurt and to increase energy. The problem with survival stress is that it takes its toll after a quick burst. You soon feel exhausted.

Although adrenaline will help you in a fight-or-flight situation, it can cause problems in less drastic environments. You may find it interfering with your ability to make good decisions, and it can consume your mental energy with distraction, anxiety, frustration, and temper.

Environmental Stress

Your surroundings can be another source of stress. A sloppy or disorganized office may make working unpleasant, especially when you can't find an important paper or phone number when you knew you had it a second ago. Constant loud or abrasive noises can be distracting—a ringing telephone, the whir of your computer, or a buzzing overhead light can all increase stress levels. To minimize it, try the following basic suggestions.

▶ Turn down the ringer on your fax machine.

▶ Lower the volume on your phone.

▶ Set up an office that operates smoothly—that is, one with a sufficiently large trash can, ample file cabinets, a place for incoming faxes, and room to store supplies.

Diet

Diet—particularly one that contains additives we don't necessarily need—also has an impact on stress. Caffeine raises levels of stress hormones. Sugars give a quick burst of energy but just as quickly make you sleepy. Salt can raise blood pressure and put your body under chemical stress.

Life Crises

Various life crises—such as the death of a spouse or loved one, divorce, or personal injury or illness—will have an impact on and can disrupt even the most effective stress management program. Obviously, the severity of the crisis will make the impact more severe. But you also need to be aware that not all life crises are negative. Marriage or the birth of a child—what most would consider to be highly positive events—can also affect your stress levels.

People

People are a major source of stress: irresponsible people, rude people, demanding people, people who don't appreciate us. Obviously, we cannot avoid all of the people in our life who bug us, but we can minimize our contact with them whenever possible, or at least brace ourselves against the effects of the encounters.

For example, if you have a co-worker who is particularly annoying because he or she steals credit for your work, you can take steps to get the word out about your work and to develop some tactics for coping with this kind of backhandedness in the office. A mentor can provide advice, as can one of the many books on career management. Here are more general steps to cut down on stress from people:

▶ Minimize contact with annoying people. Identify who causes you stress by using the stress diary described later in this chapter, and then make changes wherever possible. Ask for a transfer to a new department, cool off friendships even if people are old friends, get new suppliers, and take other steps to avoid these people.

▶ Recognize that a person's behavior is mostly self-projection and not caused by you. This is not always easy to remember, but try to keep in mind that a person who is rude to you is probably unhappy or jealous.

Symptoms of Stress

These lists provide some of the symptoms of stress. Taken alone, these symptoms may or may not be a signal of stress, but if you experience several at a time, you are probably feeling the effects of stress. Try to catch these symptoms early—as the amount of stress you are under increases, you may find it affects your ability to recognize what's going on around you, which will make it harder for you to identify these symptoms.

Short-Term Stress Symptoms

PHYSICAL

Faster heartbeat   Rapid breathing

Increased sweating   Tense muscles

Cool skin   Dry mouth

Cold hands and feet   A need to urinate

Nausea or "stomach butterflies"

MENTAL

Cloudy judgment   Reduced self-confidence

Less enjoyment   Shorter attention span

Negative thoughts   Lack of concentration

Things seem threatening,   Harder to deal with distraction
  not challenging

Long-Term Stress Symptoms

PHYSICAL

Change in appetite   Headaches

Frequent colds   Acne

Back pain   Sexual problems

Digestive problems   Exhaustion

EMOTIONAL

Anxiety   Lethargy

Worry   Insomnia or difficulty sleeping

Confusion   Reduced sex drive

Feeling out of control   Mood changes (depression,
  or overwhelmed   frustration, helplessness)

BEHAVIORAL

Talking too fast or too loud

Yawning

Fiddling, twitching, biting
   nails, drumming fingers

Defensiveness

Irritability

Aggression

Being unreasonably negative

Making more mistakes;
   being accident prone

Lack of concentration

Neglect of personal appearance

Keep a Stress Diary

Your ability to manage your levels of stress is dependent on being able to recognize when stress occurs, what causes it, and what level of stress suits you. A stress diary—a log of the stresses you experience over the course of a day—can be an effective way to pinpoint areas where you may need to reduce your stress.

You need to keep this diary for only a few days, a week at most. It doesn't have to be formal—a yellow legal pad will do just fine. And it's probably not necessary to repeat this exercise often, unless, of course, your lifestyle goes through significant changes or you are suddenly feeling your stress levels rising for other reasons. In any case, the results should give you some valuable insights.

Every hour, or at some other regular interval, record what stress you're feeling at that moment. Jot down:

▶ The time

▶ The amount of stress you're feeling—on a scale of 1 to 10, with 1 being completely stress free, and 10 being totally stressed

▶ How happy you feel

▶ Whether or not you're enjoying your work

▶ How efficiently you're working at that moment

You also might want to note particularly stressful events as they occur, along with how you reacted to the event. Take note of:

▶ The event that caused the stress

▶ When and where it happened

- The amount of stress you felt (on the 1–10 scale)
- Factors that may have made the event stressful
- How you handled the event
- Whether or not you were able to handle the stress, and if so, how you did it

After a week or so, review your diary and analyze your results. You might even want to compare your stresses with the outcomes of the projects you were working on while you were under stress. The entries in your diary will help you understand the level of stress you are happiest with, and the level of stress at which you work most efficiently. For example, you might find that an upcoming deadline gets your heart pumping and your creative juices flowing, giving you great satisfaction.

You'll also be able to track the sources of any unpleasant stress you're feeling. By recording the circumstances that made the stresses particularly displeasing, you'll begin to comprehend how your actions and other factors are influencing your stress levels. And that's the first step toward recognizing what's causing your stress and how you can manage it better.

Create a Plan for Managing Stress

Once you have determined what stress you're experiencing, you're on your way to getting it under control. Your next step is to begin to develop a plan for reducing the stress in your life.

Think of this as an action plan for managing stress. First, you need to identify each area where stress is entering and interfering with your life. These should be clear from the stress diary you've been keeping. Then, come up with the actions you can take to reduce or eliminate this stress. Later in this chapter, I discuss many of the different stress management techniques that home office workers use.

I highly recommend that you create some kind of structure around this plan, if for no other reason than that a lack of structure invites stress back into your life. It doesn't have to be an elaborate document—a simple two-column chart that notes the stress you're feeling and the action you will take to reduce it will do. Check out the sample plan to see how it's done.

Sample Plan for Managing Stress

Stress	Action
Client demands late revision on no notice	Open up lines of communication by scheduling weekly planning sessions to review ongoing work and future projects.
Phone Interruptions	Use deep breathing whenever phone interrupts important work. Hire an answering service or let machine answer the phone so I can complete important tasks.
Books and taxes are late	Hire part-time bookkeeper to keep books and handle bill paying; investigate payroll service.
Jumpy in the morning after sleepless night	Reduce amount of caffeine I drink; go to bed at 10 each night to get adequate sleep.
Street noise disrupts importrant conference call	Buy white-noise machine; investigate double-paned windows.
Kids burst into office to complain about each other; creative thoughts lost	Install "stop-go" sign on office door. Review ground rules on interruptions.
Don't feel prepared for upcoming Acme presentation	Rehearse product demonstration in front of co-workers; ask for feedback.
Can't find important papers during conference call	Clean desk to remove piles of old papers; work with consultant to create new filing system.

Get Yourself Psyched

Some people need added amounts of stress in order to get motivated and perform at peak level. Athletes are a great example of this—think of football players who pound on each other's shoulder pads, or basketball players jumping up and down and high-fiving before the big game. What they're doing is psyching themselves up—increasing their arousal levels to increase their performance.

You don't have to head-butt or let out a primal scream before a big presentation, but there are times—maybe because you're tired or uninspired—when taking certain small steps to increase your stress will benefit your ability to accomplish what you need to. Try these techniques to psych yourself up:

Focus on the importance or urgency of the task. Sometimes we fail to realize exactly how critical a certain task may be. For instance, if you're unable to make a phone call to a particular prospect, it may help you to remember that without phoning, you can't get an appointment.

Set up a challenge for yourself. This can be as simple as "Finish the bookkeeping before lunch" or "Get the name of the store's furnishings buyer." Some people even do this by creating little games for themselves— "If I get two people to say yes to me in the next hour, I win."

Use suggestion techniques. Close your eyes for a minute and begin to recite something like "I feel the energy flowing into me" or "I'm the most creative mind on the planet."

Break a large job down into smaller, more manageable elements. Small, manageable deadlines can give you greater satisfaction because you'll be aware of what you're completing, not what you're not doing.

Worrying

Worrying is a habit, just like biting your nails or tapping your foot when you're nervous. In fact, you may not even realize that you're doing it. If you worry a lot, chances are that it's because you have done it a lot in the past. And like all habits, it can be kicked. Because working at home can increase your stress level if you are not careful, it is important to examine your worrying habits.

In order to stop yourself from worrying, or at least diminish the amount you worry, you need to first understand it. Worry is your mind facing problems and trying to figure out what to do with them. Worry creates emotional stress when we think about past events or future events that are anxiety provoking. The mind is so powerful that we can upset ourselves about something just by thinking about it, as though it were happening to us right now.

Worry is part of being a human being, but it is bad if either or both of these exists—if you worry about something in the past that you can do nothing about, or if you worry about something in the future that is unlikely to happen. Even for events that are likely to happen in the future, worrying is not useful.

Tom Borkovec, Ph.D., at the Stress and Anxiety Disorders Institute at Penn State University, has created some steps for managing worry. He recommends applying one of the methods described below for a few weeks to find the one that works best for you. If, after conscientious practice, you do not notice a decline in your worrying, shift to a different method. In some cases, combining different methods may work.

1. Observe your worrying. Most of us are not even aware that we worry. So if you want to stop worrying you have to become aware of your worrying so that you can catch it as soon as it begins. By becoming aware of your worrying, you can learn to switch it off when it first begins.

2. Count your worrying. Make marks on a notepad, use a counter on your watch, or otherwise record this information. At the end of the day, write down the total, and watch this trend over a few days. This procedure is a reminder and will be useful when you apply worry reduction techniques as a means of evaluating your progress.

3. Limit the time you worry to the "Worry Period." Establish a thirty-minute worry period each day. This is a time you set aside for worrying. When you start to worry at other times of the day, remind yourself to put if off until your designated time.

These three techniques should be used in the following way: Observe your worries and catch them early, then postpone them until your worry period. To persuade yourself to do this, tell yourself that you do not have to be concerned with your worry right now, because you will attend to it during your worry period. In fact, this may actually lead you to a better solution to the problem, because your worries won't be around to distract you. Postponing worry and redirecting your focus will help reduce worry frequency and duration.

Determine What You Worry About

To determine what you worry about and to learn to notice when you worry, try the following techniques:

1. Identify the thoughts you have when you worry. Write down the exact wording that is being created in your mind—"Oh no, I'm going to miss this deadline and I'm going to lose my job and I'm going to have to move to a smaller house . . ."

2. Analyze these thoughts one at a time, and determine how logical each is and how likely it is to happen.

3. Even if the event happens, will you be able to handle it? What actions can you take to minimize its effects? Have you handled similar situations in the past?

4. Find the questions that have positive answers—that is, you believe it is likely that things will work out, or if they do not, you will be able to manage what happens.

5. For some worries, it may be useful to ask yourself what's the worst thing that could happen. Sometimes it turns out to be not so terrible, or something you could handle even if it were bad. The future is sometimes scary because it is unknown, so your ability to plan for it can make it appear much safer.

Practical Techniques for Stress Reduction

You may not be able to eliminate stress from your life, but you can reduce its impact and keep it from compounding on itself. Think of stress as if it were a dam in a flood—the more you try to hold back, the more strain you will add, and your dam will burst. But if you open a few valves, you will ease the pressure and save the day. I've put together some proven techniques— valves for your business dam—that you might want to try.

Anticipate stressful events. If you can anticipate when stress will happen, you can prepare for it and control it. As you learn more about your own personal causes of stress, you will be able to plan for them, and build in actions to alleviate stress. For example, you might be apprehensive of public speaking but have to make an important presentation in front of a client's board of directors. If you run through the presentation several times in advance, you can polish your techniques and build your confidence, thereby reducing your stress.

Reduce the importance of an event. Certain events are breeding grounds for stress because of their importance and significance to you. It could be the possibility of a major contract for an entrepreneur, or an upcoming performance evaluation for a telecommuter. The problem with big events is that they often feature elements that are out of your control, which can cause tremendous anxiety. Instead of focusing on the importance of the event, concentrate your efforts on what you can control. For a large presentation, focus on the quality of your performance, not on the potential financial rewards. Remember that you can only do the best you can and that the ultimate decision is not in your control.

Reduce uncertainty. A lack of information can hamper your ability to perform. You might not have a clear idea of where your company is heading, you might not know what clients or colleagues think of your abilities, or you may be giving yourself vague or inconsistent instructions.

To counter this, you can do two things, both of which have to do with providing you with more information. The first is to plan more effectively. Does your company have a strategic business plan or a marketing plan, or do you work in a scattershot approach. A focused plan will give you a roadmap that lets you anticipate what obstacles your business might face so that you can best handle these bumps and jostles.

The next is to ask for information you need. Do you need to know what your supervisor thinks of your work? Ask for an evaluation. Do you need help defining the parameters of a particular project? Ask for clarification. Research is another option—learning as much as you can about a person or subject can boost your preparedness and lower your stress.

Keep things in perspective. When you're under stress, it's easy to lose perspective. Minor problems can take on major significance. This, of course, makes you feel more stressed. . .which makes your problems seem worse . . . which causes more stress . . . and so on.

When you face what appears to be a huge problem, ask yourself these questions:

▶ *Is it really a problem?* Viewed a different way, many problems can be seen as opportunities to do something well or as experiences you can learn from.

▶ *Is this a problem anyone else has had?* Speak to a friend or colleague who may have experienced something similar to learn from their experiences.

▶ *Can this problem be broken down?* Take something huge and see if it can be turned into several smaller, more manageable tasks.

▶ *Can these problems be prioritized?* This helps you distinguish between what's important and what can wait.

▶ *Does it really matter?* If everything goes wrong, what's the worst thing that can happen? Will it matter three years from now or even three days from now? Seek comfort in knowing that you're doing your best.

Use time management. Your ability to use your time effectively and efficiently will have a great impact on your stress levels. The most stressful jobs are, not surprisingly, the ones in which you are under a lot of pressure and have very little control over your schedule. You might need to cut down on meetings, outsource some of your work, get an assistant, or use other time management or task organization strategies. You can read more about time management in chapter 5.

Laugh. You've probably heard the expression "laughter is the best medicine." In the case of stress management, this may be the case. William F. Fry, M.D., a Stanford University expert on the physiological effects of humor, believes that laughter may trigger changes in the body that ease pain and reduce stress. He contends that laughter can lower your heart rate and your blood pressure, and it causes your chest, abdomen, and shoulder muscles to contract, thus providing stress relief. Plus, laughter helps diffuse rage and hostility—two major causes of stress.

Laughter has a part in both your personal and your professional life. A sense of humor—the ability to see the absurdity in your daily grind and have fun in everything you do—will make you more creative, less rigid, and more open to new ideas and methods. This doesn't mean that you have to be an expert joke teller. Instead, you need to do things that amuse you and keep things light and fun when they're getting dark and dreary. Buy yourself a "joke-a-day" or "comic-a-day" calendar to give yourself a chuckle in the morning. Keep a couple of toys in your desk drawer to remind yourself of the child within you. Put a funny screen saver on your computer. Wear a silly hat when things get really tough. Remember what gives you joy, and then give it to yourself regularly.

Relaxation Techniques for Reducing Stress

When used consistently, relaxation techniques can both reduce stress and help you reach a state of mental calm. We each have our own ways of relaxing—it might be a warm bath, yoga, a long walk, or calming music. Try a number of different techniques to find out what works best for you, and then incorporate these activities into your daily life. The ones described below can be done almost anywhere at any time.

Controlled breathing. Almost all forms of stress reduction include some kind of deep breathing. That's because when you're stressed, you start to breathe irregularly by holding your breath, breathing shallowly, or sighing. If you master controlled breathing, you can incorporate it into other relaxation techniques.

Find a comfortable place with few distractions. Close your eyes and breath in slowly through your nose, taking ten to fifteen seconds to fill your lungs. Breath from your diaphragm (the muscle above your stomach), not from your chest. Slowly exhale through your mouth, and concentrate on your diaphragm contracting. Repeat this deep breathing five to ten times. Stay focused on your breathing, feeling the air going in and out of your lungs while your diaphragm expands and contracts.

Imagery and visualization. Visualization, where you use your mind to picture yourself in a place that you find relaxing and pleasant, can be a highly effective method of relaxation, especially when it's combined with controlled breathing.

Begin by closing your eyes and feeling yourself breathe. Think of a place you remember as peaceful, restful, beautiful, and happy—for example, the beach. Slowly bring your senses into the picture. Feel the sand between your toes; taste the salt from spray off the water; smell the suntan lotion; hear the roar of the surf. Put yourself deep into this imagined place to retreat from stress and pressure.

Using imagery can help you to rehearse for a big event. You might use it before an important presentation, running through in your mind everything that might occur. What does the room look like? Where will people sit? How will you sound? What will be the reaction? This mind-driven rehearsal allows you to preexperience your achievement and will give you added self-confidence.

Meditation. The idea behind meditation is to clear your mind of all thoughts for a sustained period of time. This rests your mind in many ways and has the potential to heal your body by, among other things, diverting your thinking away from problems that may be causing you stress. It gives your body time to relax and replenish itself. It relaxes your breathing, reduces your blood pressure, and can ultimately help you think more clearly with added focus and concentration.

If you want to try meditation, you could purchase one of the audiotapes, videos, or books on the market that walk you through the process, or you could attend a yoga class. Attending a class or using these tools as a guide will help you learn to quiet your mind enough to meditate. To try meditation on your own, sit comfortably against a wall with your back supported for comfort. Close your eyes, focus on your breathing, and listen to the sound of your breath. Think about your breath traveling up and down your spine or in and out of your belly button. These are two common visualization techniques that can take your mind off of your worries. Don't become frustrated if your mind wanders, just focus for as many breaths as you can. You may only want to sit for five minutes when you begin and then gradually work your way up to twenty minutes a day or longer.

Exercise. Frequent physical activity may be one of the best stress reducers around. Exercise improves the blood flow to your brain and can cause your body to release endorphins, which give you a feeling of happiness and well-being. I discuss exercise in greater depth in chapter 11.

Work/Life Balance

8

I f you're not careful, a home office can make you feel as if you should devote every waking hour to your job because your office is nearby. If this happens and your work becomes all-consuming, your personal life can deteriorate, your health may suffer, and the work you are giving it all up for may be negatively affected. In this chapter you learn how to judge whether your work/life balance is out of whack and how to realign it if it is. You will also read about a pair of successful business people and learn how they reclaimed a healthy balance between a satisfying professional life and a rewarding personal life. If your challenge is that you do not currently possess a satisfying personal life, a section in this chapter outlines how to create one for yourself.

Is Your Life out of Balance?

Ask yourself this question: If someone you meet at a party asks you about yourself, can you only answer the question of who you are with a what-you-do-for-a living answer? If the answer to this is yes, you may be suffering from shrunken life syndrome. This is a hackneyed example, but it makes the point—do you have a life beyond your work?

Another telltale sign of missing work/life balance is that for months or years you have been telling yourself that you are just busy now, but that soon all your work will pay off and you will return to a normal schedule. This is a trap that is easy to fall into. If you have been saying for more than six to twelve months that your busyness is temporary, you may be kidding yourself.

Other symptoms that you are working so hard that you leave little time or room in your life for relaxing include:

- ❱ Forgetfulness
- ❱ Frequent fatigue
- ❱ Irritability
- ❱ Lower productivity
- ❱ Physical complaints that range from aches and pains to lingering colds

Regaining Balance

If you are reluctant to cut back on the amount you work, even though you are suffering from the effects of it, some facts about the effects of working all the time may help.

- ❱ If you neglect your personal life, you will wind up with fewer good ideas and less creative input from outside sources than if you were involved in a variety of activities. A break from the office gives your brain time to think, and interaction with other people provides input that can either net good ideas directly or lead to some creative thinking on your part.

- ❱ Every movie you see, book you read, or walk you take has the potential to provide a great idea for your work, whether you are a home-based entrepreneur or a telecommuter. I developed the concept for my public radio commentaries while I was driving up to Boston. I have found loads of good ideas from reading books and seeing movies, and I usually come away from most social activity with more energy than I had before I went.

▶ A lack of a satisfying personal life also leaves you with few interesting subjects to discuss when you need to break the ice with clients or colleagues. Look at it from your perspective: would you rather do business with someone who had few outside interests and no apparent personal life, or with an interesting, vital person who could share life experiences with you.

▶ If you really need mercenary motivation to break away from work, keep in mind that lots of social activity can lead to good networking.

▶ Many health problems are related to stress and overwork. Working all the time may seem like a good path to success, but it can eventually lead to losing productivity because of illness or lowered performance.

▶ Total focus on work may have a negative impact on your personal relationships. This could mean that when you finally achieve the great success for which you are striving, you will have no one to share it with.

Get Your Life Back

Jim is a good example of a home-based worker who realized that his personal life had been pretty much buried under a workload heavier than anything he'd experienced before.

In his traditional office job as national program director for a major nonprofit organization, Jim had become used to doing too much for too little, and he even took pride in his ability to do so. "As a professional helper," he says, "I was a workaholic." But it also took a while to learn that as a private consultant, he was driving himself even harder. He began to examine his work habits in a way he never thought of doing when he worked for other people. "Finally, it got very clear, when I had unreasonable deadlines and too much work, there was nobody else to blame."

After Jim realized that he wasn't seeing enough of his wife or keeping in touch with his only son, he began to plan his work differently. "Each Monday morning when I start out my week, I think What am I doing to connect with my son? What plans do my wife and I have together?" He's careful to make conscious decisions about how to arrange his time based on what is important to him—giving these items equal importance with routine business matters such as seeing clients and making sales calls.

And as Jim accepted that he worked better when he paid attention to his personal well-being, he started doing other things to take care of himself. He doesn't kid himself that traveling on business is like taking a vacation. Jim travels between 40,000 and 60,000 miles each year—so he set some rules to ensure his comfort. He learned to take along important personal items, such as books and tapes. "It symbolizes that when I travel, I take care of myself the same as when I'm at home." In the evenings, he doesn't go to large group meals. He prefers to dine with no more than three or four people, and he doesn't even do that unless he absolutely has to: "I claim the evenings for myself: shopping, reading, paying bills—my life goes on." He also tries to maintain his routine, including exercise and meditation while traveling. When he's back at home, Jim also takes care of himself by scheduling a massage every now and then, working later in the evenings to make up for the time.

Here are the key ingredients to Jim's solution:

1. He devoted considerable time to discovering the source of his dissatisfaction. This is a universal—and universally difficult—first step. After all, we get into patterns of imbalance because we don't feel able to spend time on the intangibles.

2. Jim realized that he was the only person in control of his fate. Here is a breakthrough that most home office workers could make anew every week. You may have the feeling that your clients, customers, associates, and the bottom line are in charge of your life. But it isn't so. If you're not running your own personal life, how good a job do you think you can do running your business?

3. He developed a system for taking care of himself and his relationships with other people that fit in with his work demands. Some may balk at the idea of jotting a reminder note to write to a child in another city. But let's face it, if you find that you're not doing these

things as often as you'd like, you never will unless you incorporate it into your schedule.

4. He had a willingness to be unconventional and also to "pamper" himself. Few of us may take the trouble to bring treasured objects along on a business trip. But Jim understood that he felt much more at home—and therefore at his best—when he had his personal items with him.

False Urgency

In the movie *Postcards from the Edge*, the main character sums up her worldview with this statement: "Instant gratification takes too long." That was a hilarious line when the movie came out. Now, it pretty much describes the way most of us approach all aspects of our work.

It's easy to see how we got this way. Technology makes it possible to receive information almost instantly and to send it off to its next destination in a matter of moments. The computer brings us more data than any of us can reasonably hope to assimilate. In doing so, it makes us feel that we're always behind, no matter how hard we try to keep up. The fax machine extrudes letters, memos, invoices, and budgets, and this immediacy implies that our instant response is required on every item that appears. All this is to say nothing of overnight and priority mail services, which by their very nature and wrapper scream URGENT.

Warning Signs That Your Life Is out of Balance

It's often difficult to tell whether or not our lives are balanced between work and nonwork. In order to help you determine this, you might want to take the following quiz. Answer each question honestly.

1. Have you stopped seeing friends because it seems like a waste of your time?
2. Are family members complaining that they see too little of you?
3. Have you missed important family occasions because of work?
4. Do you see fewer movies/concerts/plays/sporting events, and so forth because of work?
5. Do you find yourself feeling bored or empty when you're not working?
6. Are you unsure of what to do with yourself when you're not busy?
7. Does relaxing make you feel guilty or nervous?
8. Do you have trouble making conversation that isn't about your job?
9. Do you work to the point where you are simply too tired to do anything else?
10. Do you have trouble saying no to work-related requests?
11. Do you evaluate your day strictly by the amount of work you accomplished?
12. Have you been wondering recently what the point of all this work is?

If you answered yes to four or more of these questions, it's time to make some changes that will help balance the demands of your work with the requirements of a healthy life. You may be sacrificing relationships and other nonwork interaction because your only satisfaction is coming from your professional life. If you've begun to suspect that you're putting too much of yourself into working and too little into living, read the next section with special care.

A Blueprint for Restoring (or Preserving) Balance

To restore balance, you need to remember that you are your most precious—and irreplaceable—resource. If you don't function well, neither will your business if you are an entrepreneur. As a telecommuter, overworking causes you to risk burnout that can hurt your hopes for career advancement and continued telecommuting.

With this in mind, treat yourself the way you would treat any indispensable business resource. You wouldn't drive your car without periodically checking the oil and taking it to the shop for maintenance. You wouldn't leave all your equipment running for hours every day with no break or downtime. Even your computer may have a screen saver to prevent burnout from continual use. Try imagining yourself as a piece of valuable and delicate equipment: your natural limits must be taken into account and should be accepted and dealt with respectfully.

Next, conjure up the vision of another person in your place and evaluate the way you treat yourself. Ask yourself if you would expect an employee to work the hours you demand of yourself, under the strain you are forced to bear. You might expect it during a busy time or for a short-term project, but even then, you would expect them to eventually request a reprieve.

With this perspective in mind, consider these suggestions for restoring balance to your life.

Stop thinking of yourself as a professional. That is, stop thinking that you're *only* a professional, forgetting that you're also a person with family, friends, and the need for exercise, relaxation, and a social life away from the job.

Make a list of the activities that give you the most enjoyment. The items on your list can range from simple pleasures—watching the birds outside your window, drinking a cup of tea in the late afternoon, working a crossword puzzle, or checking the ball scores in the sports section—to larger-scale investments of leisure time, such as: giving a dinner party, playing tennis, visiting a friend, or working in your woodshop. The point of creating this list is to identify the things that bring you joy so that you don't lose sight of them and substitute work instead. Keep this list where you can see it—you'll have a balance meter. If you glance at the list and realize that you haven't done anything on it for a while, it's time to stop and take a break.

Check your priorities. Do your activities reflect the priorities you express? Maybe you say that your priority is family and friends but find yourself spending very little time with them. This may be because you've got one set of priorities on a conscious level and an entirely different agenda at the subconscious level. Jot down your priority list and compare it with an audit of how you're spending your time.

Face your fear of nonwork. Think of something you'd really love to do—but are a little reluctant to attempt. Write down your apprehensions surrounding this activity. Taking a hard look at fear often helps to dissipate it.

Make personal time a goal. Set your sights on personal achievements when you are making your weekly, monthly, or yearly business goals. Take them as seriously as you do the goals or milestones in your business plan.

Commit yourself. If you find that you're having trouble actually getting out and doing things that are important to you, make a firm commitment that will compel you to do it. Agree to meet a friend for aerobics at the gym; set up a regular walking time two or three days a week; buy season tickets to the ball game, theater, or symphony; order bulbs from your favorite gardening catalog. This way you're committed to the exercise, the ball game, or the garden whenever the designated time comes.

Take time to relax. It's okay to do nothing sometimes. In fact, it's a good idea. If you are in a state of imbalance with work and life, chances are that your stress level is high and anxiety is a frequent companion. One of the best cures for these ailments is relaxation, so build time for it into your schedule. And to make sure that you keep the commitment to yourself, write it down on your calendar just as you would an important business meeting or conference call. And then just relax. This won't be the time for family or social obligations, and don't try to catch up on your professional reading or income tax receipts. This is time just for you. Clearing your mind this way at least once a week will give you perspective and leave you refreshed and creative.

Judith—A Case History

Neglecting to do the things you most enjoy can make you impatient and irritable, and I'm sure you'll agree that these are not moods you want to impose on your colleagues, customers, or clients. But finding a solution to this situation requires that you be flexible enough to reorder priorities and even to let go of old ideas about what is important.

Judith, a psychotherapist and clinical social worker who sees clients at her home office in Vancouver, Washington, is a case in point. She liked having the freedom to build exactly the practice she wanted and to do the kind of therapy she was most interested in.

Despite these positives, Judith found herself feeling dissatisfied much of the time. "I began to notice two things: one was that I felt extremely isolated and the other was that I felt increasingly irritable and impatient with clients." She worried that these feelings would creep out and taint the therapy process and make her less effective as a therapist.

Judith thought it over and discovered the root of her problem. She'd been spending so much time preparing to work—doing frequent household chores so that her home would always be in perfect condition for receiving patients—that she had little time left over for a personal life. "I'd sacrificed all my leisure time to working all around the practice, and I wasn't pursuing my passions of seeing films, going to art exhibits, and visiting with friends." She realized that she'd gradually substituted efficiency and competence for passion and pleasure. "I found that housework and laundry were no substitute for the things I love," she said.

Here are the steps that were key to Judith's solution:

1. She took time to sit quietly and think about how she felt. She knew that she was dissatisfied, but it was a vague sense. If she had just kept working at her old pace and in her former pattern, she would never have understood the source of her short temper and inclination to irritable behavior.

2. She devoted time to pinpointing the problem. Again, this required quiet reflection—not frenzied activity. Judith had to stop dusting furniture and washing teacups long enough to realize that doing exactly that was the heart of her problem.

3. She came up with a solution to her problem—to change her attitude about how much tidiness was required. Because she took the time to really study the problem and the solution, Judith chose the remedy that fit best for her lifestyle.

4. She changed her behavior. She chose to do less housework. But the real key was that she also changed her attitude about the relative importance of the work. You don't have to be a psychotherapist like Judith to use an open mind as one of your tools.

Building a Personal Life

Maybe you've been working so much that you think that having a personal life means walking the dog every night and doing your laundry on Saturdays. If you find yourself a little thin in the personal life department because you have devoted so much time and energy to work for so long, you might need a jump start to get you going. Here are some helpful suggestions:

Take a class. Just as you might take a class to better your business skills, sign up for one that can improve your personal life. Go for something that you've been interested in but are a little intimidated by. Try photography, or social dancing, karate, tennis, or cooking. You've got nothing to lose and only new interests and perhaps new friends to gain.

Network with a different goal. You may go to networking events all the time for your business, but make sure that professional mixers aren't the only social events you attend. On the other hand, don't neglect the opportunities inherent in these get-togethers. Networking can be personally satisfying if you approach it as a person and not just as a representative of your business. You can make friends at these events—friends who have nothing to offer your business.

Volunteer and join a committee. When you volunteer for a cause you really care about—whether it's working for your favorite museum, working in a community garden, supporting your local library, or saving stray animals—you've got a built-in emotional stake. For the less hands-on groups you may join, be sure to sign up for a committee to ensure that you actually do get involved *and* meet people with similar interests.

Talk to strangers. If you're browsing in the bookstore, picking produce at the market, standing in line to vote— whatever—take a small risk and strike up a conversation if you're near someone who seems friendly and appealing. I'm not talking about hitting on the opposite sex . . . just being friendly with someone. In fact, it can be especially rewarding if you chat with an older person. You will be amazed at the things you learn and the satisfying exchanges you will have. It's rare that you'll walk away with a new friend, but you will have expanded your universe incrementally. And it's not out of the question that you might just walk away having made a promising new acquaintance.

Instigate fun. Call a few friends (or acquaintances or like-minded clients) and suggest a picnic at a local park, a group night at a baseball game, a round of billiards at the local parlor, a movie or play you can all talk about afterward over coffee or dinner. Entertain, if you're so inclined: toss an informal dinner at your place and keep the meal low-maintenance so that you can enjoy your guests. Don't wait to be invited to do something. That method can leave you doing laundry alone every single Saturday.

Hobbies

I recently read an op-ed column in which someone claimed that nobody had hobbies anymore. That's a shame. We have an unfortunate image of hobbies—for example, someone sitting around carving a duck out of soap or putting a three-master into a bottle. Actually, a hobby is something you do just for fun, something you do not for material gain but *because you like to do it.* For the home-based worker, hobbies can be a great way to differentiate your work-related activities from your personal activities.

Just to prime the pump a bit, here's a list of hobbies you may want to consider. And remember, if something here appeals to you but you've never tried it before, you can always take a class or join a group that takes beginners.

- Cooking
- Gardening
- Reading (It doesn't have to be solitary; join a monthly book group.)
- Hiking
- Skiing
- Bird watching
- Listening to music
- Playing music
- Wine tasting
- Astronomy
- Traveling
- Sailing
- Collecting (books, pottery, fifties lunch boxes, seashells, 78-rpm records, the list is unlimited; I collect playing cards)

▶ Cultural exchanges (The Internet makes it easier than ever to meet someone from Hong Kong, Japan, Israel, wherever.)

▶ Scuba diving

There are dozens of potential hobbies and interests that I haven't listed here. Try making your own list, and see how many items you'd be interested in pursuing. If you are not sure what you'd like to do, ask family and friends for ideas. They may have memories of you as a child enjoying a particular activity that you have forgotten you like to do.

Vacations

Vacations are a vital component of a balanced life. But many, many home-based workers—entrepreneurs and telecommuters—give up on the whole notion of vacations the minute they start feeling overwhelmed by work. This is one of the great occupational hazards for those of us who work from home. The thinking seems to go that if we're not working all the time, we're not diligent, we'll risk looking unproductive to our bosses or losing our clients if we run a business.

The truth is that those who do take occasional time off are more successful in the long run than those who feel they must strap themselves to the mast and keep watch no matter what. For one thing, taking a break demonstrates that you have confidence. You know that you can remove yourself temporarily and trust that your job or your business will survive. It also sends a message that you value yourself enough to schedule time for a break. By the same token, never taking vacations suggests a desperate quality—as if you are afraid to turn away from your work for even a moment lest you lose everything.

It is true, however, that making the break from work and finding time for a vacation can be a dicey business. Here are some tips to help you schedule that time away:

Plan carefully. If you are nervous about going away, take special care in choosing a time that will have the least amount of impact on your work. For example, August is a slow time for many businesses, an ideal time to slip away without too much fallout. If a good time to go away is not clear-cut, do some research to put your mind at ease. Check trade show schedules to make sure that you will not miss important events, and ask clients or your manager when large projects are likely to be demanding your time. This will minimize the chance of you being broadsided at the last minute with a commitment that is difficult to leave behind.

Understand the vacation phenomenon. In order to make sure that you take vacations when scheduled, you need to become acquainted with one particular phenomenon: regardless of when you decide to go on vacation, your workload before you go will make you feel as though it is "a bad time to get away from your home office." It is okay to have those feelings, just simply ignore them. My trip to Spain last year coincided with a lucrative project, the deadline for this book, and a trade show that brought dozens of people to New York that I wanted to meet with. However, the trip I took with my husband was worth all of the things I missed, and it rejuvenated me so that I was able to complete higher-quality work when I returned.

Avoid living for retirement. It is tempting to put off vacations, but it is rarely advisable. Sadly, I know of many people who are retired and are now, just as they are planning on enjoying themselves, battling health problems or other challenges.

Start small. If you're nervous about going away, start by scheduling a getaway over a long weekend when others will also be taking a break.

Don't bring work. Push yourself to get work done before you leave by telling yourself that you're not allowed to take anything with you.

Ditch the beeper, cell phone, and laptop. Once you are on vacation, don't pollute your time off by being a slave to your technology. Even calling in to check messages can pollute several days of your vacation.

Keep a low profile. Don't give out a number where you can be reached unless you are truly indispensable and your co-workers or clients are likely to be faced with an emergency that only you can handle. Don't forget, even M.D.s and psychotherapists have colleagues fill in for them during absences! You might want to put a message on your answering machine that says something like "I will be out of the office from Monday, July 2, through Wednesday, July 11. Please leave a message, and I will get back to you when I return. If this is an emergency, please call my colleague John Smith at 555-5555."

Plan ahead. A few weeks before you leave, write down all of the tasks you take care of in your home office without even thinking about it, such as pulling shades down to make sure your equipment doesn't get too much sun, emptying the trash can in the employees' bathroom, and locking windows and doors at the end of the day. If staff need to get in to work while you are away, don't forget to give them keys. It is easy to overlook this item if you are used to being in the office whenever they arrive.

Think about security. Security is a big issue for home office workers who go on vacation. You have to let people know that you are out of the office for an extended period and will probably need to publicize this on your answering machine. By doing this, you create a security risk for your home and your office. We often get a housesitter. Another option is to have friends or family come to your house periodically and bring in mail, turn lights on, and generally create an aura of habitation in the house.

Plan for your return. To minimize the upheaval that you will experience upon your return, ask a trusted associate to scan your mail for bills, checks, letters from the IRS, and other important documents that arrive while you are away. Pay this person for the time that he or she spends getting rid of junk mail, writing checks, and organizing your mail so that you do not come back to a huge mess.

Short Breaks—The Shortcut to Balance

No matter how many total hours you put in during any given week, working at home nearly always affords you the freedom to take occasional short breaks. Taking advantage of this flexibility is probably the most enviable perk of working at home. Not incidentally, it's also one of the most important parts of thriving in the home office environment. These small perks, short breaks, and opportunities for independence will help you find and maintain the work/life balance that can be so elusive when you're working on your own.

If you're missing out on this wonderful perk because you get carried away with the press of business, give yourself a reminder. Post a note on your computer or close to your desk that says "Enjoy Your Freedom."

Imagine yourself lunching with a friend once a week—not talking business, just chatting and laughing. Think of the pleasure in dashing off to a movie matinee, a putting green, museum exhibition, or the gym. You may be working hard in your home office—but at least you don't have to battle the grocery store crowds on a Saturday morning or take off for your beach weekend during peak Friday afternoon traffic. Use these breaks to save yourself the hassles and crowds you can't avoid on a 9-to-5 schedule. Or simply use them to enjoy yourself.

PART THREE

Integrating Your Work Life and Private Life

Managing Family and Friends

9

When you're living with someone, working at home can intensify your relationship. This has both good and bad potential. If your relationship is on solid ground, the added time you and your spouse or partner spend together can be the best part of your home office decision. But a shaky relationship can topple under the added pressure that working at home brings. Change is the only sure thing your decision to work from home will bring to your relationship. Your ability to understand your changing role and the conflicts it may bring will have an impact on both your home life and your work life. In this chapter, I'll talk about some of the transformations you can expect, and how careful planning can help you get a grip on them. I'll also talk about some of the other "adult" relationships we have—whether they're with other relatives or with friends—and how you can set boundaries to bolster the strength of those relationships.

Making a Joint Decision

If you're living with someone, your decision to work from home can't be made in a vacuum. You need to consult with your spouse, partner, and other loved ones. Ideally, they will offer you immediate undying support. But we don't live in an ideal world, and there are many fears and apprehensions you may need to help others overcome.

This is especially true if you're an entrepreneur. Starting your own business has a high degree of risk, and although you may be ready to take that leap, others may need some convincing to leap with you. But be aware that any home office situation—whether entrepreneurial or telecommuting—upsets the family status quo. Your change of location may mean a shift in the family's lifestyle, financial security, and schedule.

Starting a home office without the support of your spouse or partner is a recipe for disaster. It will create conflict and resentment around your work and make it nearly impossible to make the adjustment. That's why you need to work *with* your spouse and loved ones and to involve them in your decision. With their support, you will be starting off on the right foot and making your work arrangement more pleasant for everyone. Here are some ways to "make your case" to your family:

Ask about their concerns and listen to their answers. It's important to unearth all their fears and apprehensions so that you can address them completely. Ask them to give you a worst-case scenario in order for you to get a clear idea of what's going on in their minds. Avoid the temptation to interrupt them to defend yourself. This is your time to ask and listen.

Do a sales presentation. Your family's fears may be based on a lack of understanding about what you do and how you are going to go about it. Spend some time assembling facts about your home office, and show them how you intend to make this effort fly. For example, a mother returning to work at a home office might want to describe how she will be able to provide child care *and* additional household income. A prospective telecommuter might want to demonstrate how he can use an extra room as an office, along with how the time saved on commuting will make him more available to his family. Again, if you've listened to your family's fears, you can use this presentation to address them accurately.

Talk about rules and boundaries. You will need to create a structure around your home office, if for no other reason than limiting the amount of upset you cause in your house. You need to address some of the misconceptions about home-based work (that you're not serious about your work; that you'll be able to be a full-time housekeeper and full-time wage earner; that you'll be available all day long for errands and other chores). I discuss these issues in greater depth later in this chapter.

Teach them about entrepreneurs. If you're starting a new home-based company, your family may be concerned that you're taking too big a risk. Explain that successful entrepreneurs are not really risk takers, that they fully examine situations and plan for multiple outcomes. Successful entrepreneurs believe in themselves and are willing to persevere when things get tough. Educating your family about this may help you to convince them that you aren't leading them down a dark road with no hope of return. Your family may also be concerned about the high failure rate of new businesses. But you can help dispel this by doing some research and looking for facts and figures that demonstrate the *success* rate of home-based businesses.

Getting Responsibilities Straight

Your decision to work from home will immediately alter your household's routine. Roles and actions that have become ingrained over time will change. Money, space, and time are all key issues that need to be addressed.

Often, the first thing that I tell people who decide to work from home is to have a planning meeting with their spouse or partner to define everyone's new responsibilities around the house so that everyone is clear about the division of labor. You need this type of clarity to avoid misunderstandings that over time can blow out of proportion. In fact, I recommend that you put all these things down in writing so that you and your spouse are perfectly clear about who is responsible for what. And remember, these need to be *joint* decisions.

Use the following list to help you create a list of items that should be covered.

Space

▶ Where will the home office be located? For example, if you are putting your home office in a room that's currently used for something else, what will the impact be?

▶ Are there potential distractions nearby that need to be moved or rescheduled?

▶ What will your hours be? Predicting a schedule is difficult, but if your office is in the bedroom or if your kids are accustomed to using your computer to play games, you may need to commit to limits on hours you will work.

▶ What are the priorities to be? If you work at the dining room table, and your spouse wants to use it for a project or to have people over, will work or personal life win out?

Money

▶ What will it cost to establish a home office?

▶ How will a home office affect household income, both in the short-term and in the long-term?

▶ What changes, if any, must be made to family spending?

▶ What money is being used for home office expenses? Will you pay for the expenses and then be reimbursed by your employer? Are the expenses coming out of a business account, or are they going to be clumped in with personal expenses?

▶ Are there any outside services that will have to be paid for, such as child care, laundry, house cleaning, and so forth?

Household responsibilities

Who will be responsible for the following tasks?

Answering the door during office hours	Cleaning the office
Child care	Clothes shopping
Cleaning the house	Cooking dinner
Cleaning the lunch dishes	Food shopping

Handling day-to-day errands

Home repair

Laundry

Office repair

Preparing lunch

Office logistics

▶ What are office hours?

▶ What do you mean by office hours?

▶ Are there any things that you and your family now do that won't be allowed during office hours?

▶ How many phone lines have to be added?

Conflict Scenarios

One reason for doing the above planning exercise is to make everyone aware of changing roles in your household and to clearly define who does what. Working at home has the potential to breed jealousy, resentment, and other negative emotions between couples if issues are left undiscussed.

I've created a series of typical work-at-home scenarios that paint a picture of possible conflicts and of how couples can deal with their changing roles. You may be able to find yourself in one of these and perhaps locate a solution to your potential conflicts.

Situation #1: The Grass Is Always Greener

Working at home with a spouse who works in a traditional office. Two-career couples face certain problems when one spouse is home-based. The most common is jealousy. The spouse who works outside the home thinks "I'm slaving away all day while my husband/wife has it easy at home" and may view the home-based worker as having less stress or pressure, because he or she doesn't have to commute or deal with the daily grind of office politics. At the end of the day, the commuting spouse might want to get home and relax, to unwind from the stress of the outside world.

On the other hand, the home-based partner may be jealous, because his/her spouse gets to leave the house every day, engage in social interaction with co-workers, go to office parties, and so on. Often, this person also feels put-upon by the other, who assumes that home-based workers have time to run errands and handle all household chores. At the end of the day, the stay-at-home spouse may want to get out after "being cooped up in the house all day."

Resolutions

▶ Spend some time every night to go over your day and share your successes and look for support for your failures. This will make each person aware of what the other is doing and will keep you from making unreal assumptions. Use this time to communicate and acknowledge each other for the work that each of you is doing. Try to avoid battles of one-upmanship.

▶ Review your household responsibilities to see if they still work. If the commuting member wants you to take on a specific task or errand during the day "because you're home anyway," respond that you'd be happy to do it after work hours, just as he/she would. You can also look for ways to share household errands and chores—perhaps the commuting partner can pick up dry cleaning during his/her lunch hour, and the stay-at-home partner can wait for the plumber. Or you can leave these chores until after work hours, when you can do them together.

▶ Show flexibility in your social life by taking turns coming up with ideas for entertainment. Rent videos and pop a bag of popcorn some nights, but also get tickets to the opera or symphony.

▶ Build on the arrangement by having the spouse who works outside of the home run errands such as going to the post office and other tasks that are located near his/her workplace. In return, the work-at-home spouse can grocery shop during off-peak hours or take care of other responsibilities that are closer to home.

▶ Communicate. If you need to work late, give your spouse a few hours of notice instead of just refusing to leave your desk when he/she returns home from work. This will eliminate the situation in which a spouse comes home from work with a great idea of heading out to a movie and dinner, only to find a work-at-home spouse glued to the computer.

Situation #2: I Don't Want You Here

Working at home with a spouse who's at home but not working. This is a common scenario when a breadwinner opts for a home office career and the other partner is a homemaker. This often sets up a turf war, where the homemaker suddenly feels as if the working spouse is intruding in his/her domain.

Sometimes the opposite is true. The stay-at-home partner may be relieved that his/her spouse will be around more "to help out around the house." This often occurs when there's a young child in the house, and the caregiver assumes that the home office spouse will be available for changing diapers or for twenty minutes of baby-sitting "while I run to the store."

Resolutions

▶ Set well-defined boundaries. Clearly determine what working at home means to you. You may need to set office hours and keep them, spelling out what is an acceptable interruption and what is not. If you have children, you will have to do this (see chapter 10); often, you have to do it with your spouse as well.

▶ Be flexible. Working at home does not have to be rigid. Sure, you can change the baby's diaper sometimes or take ten minutes to look at a leaky toilet. You just need to be clear that these are occasional tasks that can be done *when you have the time* and are not part of your regular work-time responsibilities.

▶ Respect each other's space. Retired couples often find themselves at odds because they've never before had to spend long periods of time together. The same goes for traditional office workers who suddenly start working from home. Don't clean the office unannounced, and don't start to fix the sink in the middle of dinner preparation.

▶ Watch your moods. Couples who are at home together are especially susceptible to each other's moods. If you're feeling grumpy or angry because of something that happened in the office, try not to bring it into your home life.

Situation #3: Whose Office Is This?

Working at home with a spouse who works from home. Couples who work at home together have the potential to distract each other and get on each other's nerves. They can find it hard to draw the line between what's going on at work and what's going on at home. When your spouse is around you all the time, you may find yourself having to share every setback and triumph immediately, even if the timing isn't right.

Resolutions

▶ If possible, have separate offices. This may not be an option if you're constrained by space. But if you can, there is no greater "do not disturb" boundary than a closed door.

▶ Plan early and often. I know one couple who discuss their daily plans over breakfast. This way, they know who'll be in the office when, whether there are any important meetings to expect, and so forth.

▶ Don't keep a scorecard. One of you may have to do all the household chores one week while the other prepares a major project. Be resolved that it may happen, and you may be able to avoid resentment.

▶ Spend some time apart doing what you each enjoy. Take a class. Go to a movie or dinner with a friend. Have some quality "private" time.

▶ Don't inflict your mode of operation on your spouse. Remember that you have your own way of working and that you must entitle your spouse to his/her own way too, even if you don't agree with it.

Situation #4: Hey, Let's Start a Business

Working at home together. Couples who start their own companies together have many of the same problems as the couple in Situation #3. But they also need to watch out for the roles that they define for each other, because they may not be the roles each partner wants to play. For example, if one person had previously been the dominant family earner, he/she may try to recreate that role and "boss" the other partner around. This can cause significant resentment and conflict that pours out of the office and into the home.

Resolutions

- Clearly define each of your roles in the company. Be sure each partner is clear on what he/she will do in the company. There's no problem with taking advantage of each other's strengths, but it's good to avoid pigeonholing by past experience.

- Do something together that shakes up the way you relate. If one person usually runs the show, spend a weekend doing something the other person is good at; take turns being in charge.

- Be careful not to reinforce each other's bad habits. Have a trusted third-party adviser (your CPA, attorney, or a home-business consultant) give you an unbiased view of your strategy and ideas.

- Plan work and home duties. You should be clear who will pick up the kids *and* who will lead a meeting.

- Express your feelings instead of getting mad. If you don't like the way your spouse reacts to your ideas during brainstorming sessions, say so. Always try to put things in terms of how the action makes you feel, rather than in terms of what your spouse has done wrong.

10 Ways to Clearer Communication

Marriage counselors and relationship experts will tell you that communication is the most crucial element to a growing, evolving marriage. As a home-based worker, your communication skills will be tested every day because you and your spouse will be seeing a lot more of each other. Of course, many volumes have been written about this, and I'd encourage you to read as much as you can on the subject. In the meantime, you might get some benefit from these tips.

1. Be clear about what you need **and be sensitive to the needs of others.** It's often difficult for people to say what they need, if for no other reason than that they're not clear themselves. If you want to find out what your spouse needs, you may have to ask.

2. Don't interrupt. When a discussion gets heated, we often find it necessary to defend ourselves or our position. But interrupting can be demeaning, and it takes away another person's power. It also connotes that you're not interested in what he/she is saying.

Avoid "Superperson" Syndrome

We often receive the message that "we can have it all." Advertisements, television, movies, and magazines bombard us with images and advice that make us believe that we can easily work from home, have a loving relationship with our spouse and family, cook gourmet meals every night, go to the beach on a moment's notice, keep the office and the house clean, attend PTA meetings, clean up the environment, and maybe save mankind from space aliens too.

Of course, you can't.

In particular women returning to work fall prey to this syndrome, and when they are returning to work in a home office, the chances are even greater that they'll feel compelled to take on too much. The stress and strain this causes often begins to fray the edges of a happy marriage.

If you find this happening to you, you might want to look at ways to delegate certain household chores that you've felt compelled to do but may not enjoy. A service can be called in to clean the house *and* the office. You can hire someone to come in and prepare a week's worth of meals for you and your family (keep the meals in the freezer and thaw them with a quick zap of the microwave). If mowing the lawn becomes a burden, hire a gardener.

The bottom line is that you need to set priorities about what's important to you. Yes, there's a cost involved. But you'll have extra free time to enjoy your marriage and have fun with your spouse.

3. Use "mirroring techniques" to listen. When you use mirroring, you repeat back to the person what you think you heard, so that you can be clear on what was said and he/she can be clear that you heard it properly. Mirroring forces you to be more attentive and interested in what the other person is saying.

4. Know your communication tendency. People typically fall into one of two categories: fixers and sharers. Fixers want to immediately solve whatever problem somebody has. Sharers want to share their problems but are not necessarily looking for solutions. Sharers don't like it when fixers try to repair their problems, and fixers often grow impatient with sharers' sharing. Know what camp you fall into so that you can temper your tendencies.

5. Don't judge. Trust is the basis of any strong relationship. You can accept someone else's ideas and opinions in an honest, caring way, even though you may not agree with what he/she is saying. But disagreeing does not give you permission to put someone down or disempower him or her.

6. Strike a balance between positive feedback and negative feedback. Some people tend to tell others only what they're doing wrong and to ignore what they're doing right. But positive feedback (what you like about something) makes negative feedback (what you dislike) more palatable and honest.

7. Acknowledge success and effort. Tell your spouse how proud you are of him/her when something good happens. Don't stop there. Let your spouse know how much you appreciate his/her hard work, and what it means to you as part of the family. There's nothing like a good pat on the back.

8. Understand the power of compromise. A disagreement does not have to end in one person "winning." A successful relationship is based on give-and-take. If you determine the outcome you both want from a given situation, you can work together to get there.

9. Get out of your head. Sometimes we let the brain get in the way of feelings, but feelings are okay, too. It's important to be able to share our full range of feelings with those we love and care about. Anger, sadness, disappointment, and frustration are just as valid as joy, elation, and happiness.

10. Respect and empathy go a long way. It's important to understand each other's points of view, even when they're in conflict with our own. Being able to recognize that there are other valid opinions on a subject makes us open to change and progress.

Setting Boundaries with Family and Friends

No matter how hard you try, there will be family members and friends who don't take your work seriously because you don't work in a traditional environment. It happens to me all the time—even after years of working at home, my family and friends occasionally treat me as if I'm not working, just because my office is in my apartment. Your sister might drop in unannounced for coffee because "you're always home." An old friend might want to sleep on your couch for a week, or one might be disappointed when you can't meet him for lunch. Or perhaps a neighbor wants you to drop something off with the mailman when he arrives, because "you're home."

You may encounter the same or similar treatment. The way to decrease it is to train your family and friends that your home office is as valid as any "traditional" workplace. I recommend taking the following steps.

Constantly reinforce your working situation. When friends call you in the middle of the day and you're on another call, say "I'm on with a client; can I call you back tonight?" If a family member calls with a nonurgent request, say that you're busy with a deadline and you'll get back to him or her later. These are accepted practices in the workplace, and by saying them, you are reinforcing your work/life boundaries.

Let people know that you have work hours. Just as you don't want clients to call you at home at 10 P.M., you need to let your friends and family know when you are "at work." I sometimes ask people who call me socially to do so after 9 P.M.

Always refer to the place where you work as your office. You don't work from home. You work from an office in your home. And that office is just as valid as one in a big corporate center.

Go to the door to answer neighbors' requests with a portable phone to your ear. Talk into the phone to a business associate (whether there's one there or not) whenever neighbors come to your door with a request. You can even mouth to them that you'll get back to them, or hold up a finger to indicate that you're in the middle of important business. Instead of calling them back in five minutes, call back after dinner and apologize for the delay saying you didn't have a minute to spare. They'll get the message.

Dress for work. Media images may tell you it's okay to stay in your pajamas all day when you work from home. But dressing for work creates a professional image that will be a signal to your family that you are "in the office" and "ready for work." I don't mean that you have to wear a suit and tie every day, with the occasional casual Friday. But it does mean that you should always look neat and clean and professional.

Give specific "business" reasons for turning down requests. When someone approaches you with an unwelcome request on your time, turn him or her down by saying something like "I'd love to, but I have a major client presentation that day," or "Sorry, but I'm just finishing up a proposal." The message you're trying to convey is that your office is a place of work.

Answer your business phone professionally. Even if you have only one line, answer it in your business voice during work hours. Say hello, and the name of your company or your name. This says to the caller that you're at work, not sitting around watching the soaps.

Confront the problem head-on. People may not realize that you work hard, because they don't know what you really do. Sit down with your friends and family and explain to them how hectic your days are. This blow-by-blow account will help them realize that you run a legitimate business. Then set some guidelines with them about when it's okay to call and when they're interrupting you.

Children and the Home Office

10

Many people begin working from home because they're looking to combine parenthood with their career. In fact, studies regularly show that many parents would stay at home with their children if they could, and a home office gives them a chance at this freedom. But this also creates a juggling act. Both children and your business demand a great deal of attention—often at the same time. You don't want to be put in a position where one has to suffer. On the other hand, you have a unique ability to convey to your children every day the joy and satisfaction you get from your job.

As a home-based worker, you will need to consider your child care options—will you do it yourself or will you hire someone to help you? You also need to create rules and guidelines around your home office so that both you and your children are able to separate the working you from the parenting you. This chapter gives you some information that may help you with this tricky task.

Mixing Child Care and the Home Office

If you have children and decide to work from home, how you care for your kids will be one of your most critical decisions. Child care options vary greatly. Many parents rely on full-time baby-sitters, nannies, and other child care professionals, whereas others are able to carve out time for their children, for themselves, and for their business. It's important that you come up with something that fits your budget, your needs, and, most important, your children's needs.

Full-Time Child Care

In an ideal world, you will want to hire full-time help for your children. And if you are serious about starting a home-based business or telecommuting, then I highly recommend that you investigate outside child care options—whether a full-time baby-sitter, nanny or au pair, a day care facility or preschool, or part-time help for after-school hours. If you are a corporate telecommuter, this will most likely be a requirement.

This option is taken even by parents whose primary reason for working at home is a desire to spend more time with their children. The reason is simple—even with a full-time caregiver, parents get to spend more time with their kids. When child care is in the house, parents can have lunch with their kids or take breaks to play with them for a few minutes. And when parents use day care, they get more time because without a commute, they can drop their kids off later and pick them up earlier.

Full-time help can be expensive. If you are just starting up your business or need your full work-at-home income to make ends meet, then full-time child care is probably not an option for you.

Part-Time Child Care

If you can't afford or don't want to hire someone full-time, investigate part-time child care. You might want to have someone come in to watch your kids for a couple of days a week or for a few hours each day. In either case, you're buying yourself some uninterrupted time to devote solely to your work.

If you have school-age children, part-time care is an extremely viable option to help you get in a full eight-hour workday. You get uninterrupted time at work while the children are in school. Your part-time baby-sitter can pick up the kids and watch them for the afternoon.

No Child Care

Having preschoolers at home can create a difficult and stressful work situation. Still, some people are able to manage it. It means that you'll be working with preschoolers underfoot, or that you'll be trying to squeeze in a couple of hours of work before they wake up, while they're napping, or after they've gone to sleep.

Be aware that you'll find it quite hard to get in any more than three to five hours of work a day. You will also have to prioritize your non–child care, nonwork activities, such as housecleaning, laundry, or cooking. You may find yourself making business calls while Barney is on in the background (so it may pay to be up front with clients so that they know your situation).

Once your children are in school, you'll be able to take advantage of those hours for your business. Older children (in junior high or older), may be able to care for themselves during nonschool hours and leave you alone to work (see "Set Ground Rules" on page 161).

Other Child Care Options

If hiring someone to take care of your children is not financially feasible, there are other low-cost or free options you might want to try.

Child care co-op. A co-op is a neighborhood program where parents can earn credit for watching other people's kids—credit that can be turned into baby-sitting time for their kids when they need child care. Here's an example of how it works: You watch someone's child on a Saturday afternoon for five hours when you're spending time with your own kids, and get a five-hour credit in your account. When you need some uninterrupted work time, you can cash in your credit to have someone watch your kids. Co-ops require a lot of organization and vigilant record keeping, and the person who sets it up and coordinates it usually receives credit for time spent coordinating.

You Can't Always Do It All

Mary is a freelance copy editor who recently had her first child. During her pregnancy, she worked on projects into the beginning of her ninth month. Her idea was to stay home with her daughter during her first year, take a three-month "maternity leave," during which she would not take on any projects, and after that, maybe take on an occasional project that she could complete while her daughter was napping or asleep at night. This extra fifteen or so hours of work each week would let her stay in touch with her publishing contacts and give her enough work to keep her skills in shape. And, after all, it was *only* fifteen hours a week.

Then reality sunk in. Mary soon realized that raising an infant can be exhausting and all-consuming. When her daughter was six months old, Mary took what she thought was a simple copyediting assignment . . . the kind of thing she could finish off in a couple of hours. But it wasn't that easy. "At first I was going to work while Rachel was napping, but I was so tired I couldn't concentrate, and besides, I wanted to use that time to nap myself," she said. "So I tried working at night after she went to sleep, and that didn't work either, because that was the only time of the day I had to myself, and I wanted to keep it. My priorities were my baby, myself, and then my work, but it seemed like I only had time for two of the three."

Mary realized that she had a choice to make: either stop working, or find some alternative. "My work is important to me, and I didn't want to give it up," she said. "The first thing I did was map out what I needed to do to care for Rachel, care for myself, and care for my work. In order to do my work successfully, I needed two to three hours of uninterrupted time each day. So I hired a fourteen-year-old who lived down the block to come in two afternoons a week to

> watch Rachel, and I used those four hours to take on a cou-
> ple of simple jobs. I then enlisted the help of my husband,
> who took over bathing and putting Rachel to bed every
> night, and I used that hour a day for my personal quiet time.
> It refreshed me enough that I was able to get in another two
> hours or so of work a few nights a week. That brought me
> up to ten uninterrupted work hours . . . which is right now
> what I feel I can handle. It's been a slower process than I
> thought it would be, but that's what I need."

Baby-sitting trades. This is a less formal version of a co-op. Essentially, you set up a reciprocal baby-sitting arrangement with another work-at-home parent.

Enlist the help of your older children. Have your older children pitch in around the house by watching their younger siblings. This also teaches responsibility.

Hire an adolescent baby-sitter. Of course, you want to entrust the welfare of your kids only to someone in whom you have confidence, but because you will be in the house, you might consider hiring a high school student to watch your child a few hours a day. Students charge less than other part-time or full-time child care providers.

Training Your Child Care Provider

You have to set ground rules with your children, and you also need to do it with your child care provider, as the following story illustrates.

Elise runs a successful advertising agency from her home office. It was the birth of her son, Richie, that gave her the impetus to start her own company, because she wanted to continue her rising career but still be close by to be there for her son. "I didn't want to leave the house at eight o'clock and come home at seven o'clock just in time to put my son to bed. I wanted to spend more time with him and be a part of his life while also expanding my career."

Elise even set up her office as a separate area of her home, with a separate entrance in order to create a distinct boundary between her office and her home. Then, after an extensive search, she hired a full-time baby-sitter for her then toddler son.

"What I failed to do was set strict ground rules with Lorna, Richie's nanny," Elise said. "She was an older woman who had never worked for a home-based working mom before. She assumed that since I was technically at home, I was there to take care of whatever she needed. She regularly walked into my office while I was on important phone calls, and would interrupt me with basic questions like 'what should Richie have for lunch?' or 'we're going to the park.' She soon started bringing Richie down to my office because 'he wanted to see his mother.' It was when she did this in the middle of a very sensitive presentation that I realized I had to put a stop to it."

While Elise correctly planned and implemented her home office, she neglected to adequately train her nanny. This meant that she now had to come up with a way to make it clear when it was okay to interrupt her and when it wasn't. "Businesswoman that I am, I sat down and created an action plan so that Lorna and I could make this work." Here's what Elise did:

1. While her husband watched Richie, she sat down with Lorna and clearly explained what she did for a living. "It turns out, Lorna was pretty unaware of what I was doing in my office; she actually thought it was some kind of hobby."

2. She set ground rules for what constitutes an interruption and when it's okay just to visit. "I had to let her know that the call was mine, not hers. That it was okay to interrupt in case of an emergency, and what an emergency meant."

3. She told Lorna that if she was in doubt about whether or not it was okay to visit the office, she could call first. (Elise had separate home and business lines.)

4. She mapped out time each day that she would spend time with Richie with Lorna. "We ate lunch together a couple of times a week, and instead of a coffee break, I scheduled a Richie break."

5. She started reviewing her schedule with Lorna every morning. "It was important for Lorna to know my daily schedule, whether I had any important appointments or even any major phone calls. This way, Lorna could plan her day as well. It took maybe three minutes each morning, but everyone was now clear on what to do."

Introducing Your Child to Working from Home

As I made clear in the previous chapter, your decision to work from home can't be made in a vacuum. Your children, no matter how old they are, will have many questions about what you're doing, and you should be prepared to answer them.

Here are some of the things you should expect to cover:

Why you'll be working at home. Remember that this still isn't the norm, and that your kids may not know other parents who have a home office. Take the time to tell them why you made your decision—for example, you believe that you can be more creative at home without making a long commute each day; you've come up with an idea that is exciting to you, and you are building a business; or you want to be able to spend more time with your family. Determine your reasons, and then explain them clearly and in a positive light to your kids.

Why you'll be at home and not be available to them. Your children might be excited that you'll now be at home most of the time, but you need to explain that you'll be working just as you did when you went to the office every day. Stress that you will be more available and will be able to spend more time with them . . . just not all your time. This is a particularly critical issue for the full-time mother who is returning to work at a home office.

What this will mean in terms of child care. If you're hiring a full- or part-time baby-sitter, you will need to explain what this means, especially because you'll still be at home.

How things around the house might change. A home office may mean that an area of the house is suddenly off-limits. Or you may have to change a playroom into an office. Or your kids may have to pitch in more around the house (no more toys in the hallway, because clients might visit; kids may have to fix their own snacks; etc.).

What rules to expect. You'll need to set ground rules for your kids and the office, and you need to explain these early on (see page 161).

Being a Child-Friendly Home Worker

Through having a separate home office, you may find it relatively easy to make the physical distinction between home-based worker and parent-at-home, but you may find it much harder to make the mental and emotional distinction. But if you fail to do this, you run the risk of confusing and alienating your children, which is exactly what you want to avoid. Here are a few steps that you can take to make this transition easier.

Do not consistently make yourself physically available to your kids without being emotionally available also. You won't enhance your relationship with your kids if you are present in the house but always tied up on the phone or at your computer. This kind of unavailability makes kids feel unimportant. Be sure that there are times when you are completely available to your kids.

Find the time to get involved in your kids' activities. One of the joys of home office living is the flexibility it provides you in terms of scheduling. Maybe you can coach your daughter's little league team? Or chaperone your son's school field trip? Take advantage of this flexibility to give time to your kids that you might not otherwise be able to give.

Give your children your time in other ways. Take your kids with you when you go out on a quick business errand—such as a trip to the bank or the office supply store—so that they can participate in things you do for your office.

Let your children see what you do. Let your kids come into your office to see what you do for a living. Show them a recent proposal. Let them see a finished project. Share your excitement about your work with them, so that they can see how much you enjoy what you're doing. Give them a chance to share in your successes.

Watch out for guilt. It's fairly common for work-at-home parents to feel guilty about not being with their kids while they're in the office . . . and then to feel guilty about not working while they're with their kids. Resolve yourself to knowing that the money you're earning while working at home is important to your child's welfare. Plus, by working at home, you're giving time and joy to your child that you wouldn't be able to give if you were in a more traditional setting.

Keep office tensions in the office. When you work from home, it's easy to have work issues spill over into your home life. Children pick up on tension and stress quickly, but you can't expect them to understand your adult concerns. Be aware of what you're feeling, and if a client has just angered you or if you're late on a project, be extra careful not to take it out on your children.

Creating an Office-Friendly Child

Setting boundaries with your children is a crucial part of home office parenting. Your kids need to know what behavior is acceptable and what is not. As I mentioned earlier, rules are crucial to communicating the importance of your home office to your children. If you are clear and consistent, your kids will soon be able to understand what's okay to do around your office and what's not. These tips will help you out in this area.

Set ground rules. If your kids are old enough to understand rules about the home office, establish guidelines for them regarding your business, such as:

▶ *When it is okay to approach you.* Make yourself available to them at certain times of the day, and make it clear that you are not *always* available. It should rarely be okay to interrupt you when you're on the phone.

▶ *What is an emergency.* Obviously, it should be okay to interrupt you in case of an emergency. But what constitutes an emergency? You might want to come up with some emergency and nonemergency scenarios so that your kids will be clear on this point.

▶ *Use traffic control techniques.* Create some kind of symbol that you can put on your office door to indicate when you can't be disturbed. Some parents have had success using a stop/go sign. You might even ask your kids to design it, so that they can be involved in the process.

▶ *Don't answer the office phone.* Your children should not be allowed to answer your office phone, or to use it for their personal calls.

Stick to the rules. It's important to be clear about rules, and then to stick to them. If, for example, you let your kids interrupt you or come into your office without knocking first, they will soon expect that. It's not that your rule is being ignored . . . it's that you've set a new rule (interruptions are okay) and your kids are just following it. And once bad habits such as interruptions take hold, they're hard to break.

Don't expect too much of younger children. They may not be able to understand the concept of not interrupting you while you're in the office. Show some flexibility and understanding.

Expect to be tested. Older children, especially, will test the boundaries you've established for your home office. They may make noise, interrupt you, be surly to clients, or act out in other ways. As long as the guidelines you have established for them are clear and fair, be firm with them.

Learn to say no and mean it. There are plenty of people who can't say no to their children. If you're one of them, and if you want to keep working from home, then you need to start getting into the habit of saying no *now*. This is especially crucial in setting limits around your office.

Don't turn your kids off from work. If you complain about your clients all the time, or talk about how much you hate your work, or bring other troubles home, your children will pick up on it immediately. Over time, they'll begin to associate going to the office with something bad, and that's probably not what you want to convey.

Creating a Child-Friendly Office

When you have children around the house, you have to take special care in designing your office space. Simply making the office off-limits is not okay. Many children won't understand this, and it does nothing more than create this big dark secret about what's behind the office door. There are steps you should take to make your office more friendly to your children, while preserving the importance of your work.

Install a separate phone line for your business. This is priority number one. Use this second line for business only. It is the number that goes on your business cards, and it is the number that you share with your clients. Avoid the temptation to have this line ring or be answerable where your house phone is located. It should ring and be answered only in your home office. That way, when a call comes in, either you answer it, or you let your business answering machine pick it up. If you need mobility or access to other parts of the house while you're on a business call, get a 900-MHz cordless phone with a large range.

With this setup, you won't have to carry on a business conversation while your kids are underfoot. It creates a firm distinction between your office activities and your home activities. Plus, it's much easier to explain to your children that the phone that rings only in the home office is not to be answered by anyone but you.

Find a safe place for all documents. The lure of an unfinished project is captivating to curious children, but you have to take responsibility for keeping documents safe. Place important papers on a high shelf, or in file drawers that have a lock and key. You don't want to learn the hard way by presenting a client with a document complete with grape-jelly fingerprints.

Childproof your office. If you have toddlers, you know how they can get into almost anything. Take the same care in childproofing your office as you take with the rest of your home. Put locks on all drawers and cabinets. Cover outlets with safety covers. Hide computer and other electrical cords. Get down on your hands and knees to look for dangerous areas from a child's point of view. Make sure that all tall bookshelves and cabinets are stable or firmly bolted to the wall. Keep small, swallowable objects out of reach, especially anything shiny. Remove any potted plants or other decorative items that are dangerous if eaten. Lock potentially hazardous objects (scissors, the razor knife you use to clip articles, your stapler) in a desk drawer—and don't leave the keys in the lock! Be aware that accidents do occur.

Childproof your computer. There is nothing quite so tempting to small hands as your computer. And, of course, it's probably the one piece of equipment that they shouldn't be touching. You want to make it off-limits if you can. A variety of computer security software packages allow you to "password-protect" your computer: in order to get the system to operate, you need to enter your password. This will keep your kids from accidentally getting at sensitive business files (and possibly erasing them). You can also use this kind of protection for individual computer files.

If your computer is the only one in your house with an Internet connection (and your kids are using it to do their homework), be sure to install software such as Cyber-Sitter that makes non-child-friendly web sites off-limits. These programs contain a list of verboten sites (everything

"Take Your Children to Work" Day

For the past several years, there's been a lot of publicity around "Take Your Daughter to Work" Day, which has now evolved into "Take Your Children to Work" Day. It's a great way for children to learn about what their parents do. It teaches them about the job market and also lets them learn about other careers. Just because you work in a home office doesn't mean that you can't take advantage of this special occasion. Here are some things you can try:

▸ *Take your child to a client meeting:* Take your child along with you to a client's office so that he or she can learn what you do for the client, as well as what your client does. Obviously, first clear this with the client.

▸ *Hire your child as your receptionist for the day:* Use this special day to involve your child in your workday. Teach him or her how to answer the phone professionally . . . maybe even come up with a script your child can use in order to answer correctly ("Hello, Acme Exterminators. May I help you?").

▸ *Have your child invite friends over for an office tour:* Just because you're a one-person office doesn't mean that kids can't learn from or be inspired by you. Let them see an entrepreneur in action. Prepare a little presentation that shows them what you do. Convey the excitement of owning your own business and working from home.

from mature subject matter to violent content to pornography) and make them inaccessible. If you want to view these sites, you can bypass the software through password process. Your Internet service provider should be able to supply you with this software or tell you where to get it.

Last, be sure to back up all your computer files regularly. This will make it easier to recover from an unintentional child-caused crash.

Set up a separate "kids" desk. It's nice to have a separate kids area of your office for times when your child visits you at work. For preschoolers or other young children, put a small desk off to the side that's their work area. Equip it with a toy or old phone so that they can "make business calls" (and not try to use your business phone). Put one of your extra calculators on the desk so that they can press buttons (a fascination for toddlers). Have a stack of scratch paper and a desk-set filled with crayons.

PART FOUR

........·..··.

Health

Exercise, Sleep, and Food

11

I
f you think that you're too busy to get regular exercise, eat healthy foods, or get regular sleep, you may want to reconsider. As a telecommuter or home-based business owner, you ought to be as vigilant about scheduling meals, sleep, and exercise as you are about attending business meetings.

Home offices provide more flexibility than corporate dwellings, and this freedom can lead to days that start at 6 A.M. and finish up after the 11 P.M. news, when you sit down to do just one more thing. This flat-out work regime is often coupled with hastily grabbed meals and lots of snacks. A pattern of sedentary living can also develop because breaking away from work to take a walk or go to the health club is a challenge when you are not already out of the house. But healthy habits are as vital to your business success as they are to your good health. This chapter shows you how to eat well, get sufficient sleep, and exercise regularly. Practical tips show you how to accomplish this within your busy schedule.

Getting Exercise—or Building Up Your Assets

Investing time in exercise is like investing money in your business: if you don't do it, after a while you won't have much to work with. And I'm not just talking about buns of steel or rock-hard abs, although those may come over time. In a much more immediate sense, exercise improves your day-to-day work performance and effectiveness. Besides maintaining general fitness, it will help ward off fatigue and will allow you to work productively for more hours a day. First, let's take a look at other direct daily results that you will gain from doing some kind of regular exercise.

Exercise Can Make You Smarter

The job of your cardiopulmonary system, your heart and lungs, is to pump oxygen into your blood and to then pump the blood around to all the vital places in your body that need it to stay healthy and operate efficiently. As you can imagine, your brain is one of the major destinations for this busy blood. Your gray matter makes up only 2 percent of body weight, yet it uses 25 percent of all the oxygen and blood sugar, or glucose that you take in. But when you're sitting at your desk, your lungs breathing quietly, your heart at rest, you are sending less oxygen to your brain than when you're exercising and giving the heart and lungs enough of a workout to encourage blood flow to the brain.

After a few hours of sitting at your desk without a break, your brain activity naturally slows because blood and oxygen are in lower supply. The practical effect of this situation is that you have a harder time remembering things, coming up with new ideas and solutions, and staying alert. But this will become less of an issue with proper exercise, because you'll be sending more oxygen to your brain.

Working Smarter, Not Harder

Dana Gramling is staff trainer at the Watergate Hotel's Sport and Health Club in Washington, D.C. For several years he has been teaching Washington's best minds how to improve their bodies. He advises working out in the morning if possible, because your energy, alertness, and metabolism are all enhanced by exercise. Starting the day with all systems go may enable you to function better and be smarter all day long. You also may be more likely to maintain a morning exercise regimen over a long period of time because your workout will be complete before business pressures develop and tempt you to forgo your workout. Gramling reminds his clients that exercise should be as much a part of a productive day as sleeping, eating, and making business deals.

> **H**ave you ever wondered why people in long meetings seem to have so few good ideas? Their brains are literally oxygen-deprived because they've been sitting down too long.

Ever notice how much more you yawn when you've been sitting slumped in a chair for an hour or two, how much of an effort it seems to rouse yourself? If you're a habitual nonexerciser, these occasions are probably fairly frequent. Here's why: Lack of exercise allows your support muscles to weaken and waste away, encouraging slumping and poor posture. When your body is slumping and you are yawning, your heart rate is down and so is your blood flow. Once again, the brain is being cheated out of oxygen. Hence, you're half-conscious instead of fully awake and alert. If you've been thinking lately that you're out of fresh ideas or that you're bored with your work, you could just be suffering from a lack of exercise.

And don't forget that without exercise, your body's metabolism stays lower and you wind up burning fewer calories in the course of a day. The bottom line—and I do mean it both ways—is that more and more of what you eat turns into body fat.

The tricky thing about exercise is that you may not crave it the way you crave food and sleep. In fact, a majority of Americans apparently don't

> **A** recent National Sleep Foundation study of first-year nurses working twenty-four-hour shifts found that when the nurses took half an hour away from their limited sleep time and devoted it instead to regular exercise, they were actually more alert and performed their jobs better than those nurses who'd had the extra half-hour of sleep.

crave it at all, because 60 percent don't do anything regularly. That doesn't mean that they're getting away with it. The body does ask for exercise, but the messages are a lot more subtle than the signals for sleep and food. Messages may come in the form of assorted aches and pains, increased stress, breathing difficulties, or, at the most extreme, cardiac and circulatory problems.

Exercise—The Basics

An ideal exercise plan will train both your cardiovascular system and your muscles. There are many types of exercise that provide both kinds of workout so that you don't have to be a runner or take an aerobics class to get these benefits. Visit your doctor to check out your overall health before beginning any exercise regimen, and then choose a type of exercise that you enjoy and that fits your lifestyle. Convenience is key to sticking with an exercise plan. For example, if you have to travel across town to a health club to exercise, you may not be inclined to go regularly. Instead, choose something you can do locally, such as swimming at a local college or high school pool or speed walking. Also, try to engage in an activity you enjoy, such as dancing, hiking (if you are lucky enough to live near the woods), or playing tennis.

If you have attempted exercise regimens before and have failed to stick to them, try scheduling your workout with a friend or a group. If you join a walking club, for example, or make arrangements to play tennis with someone, the pressure of keeping the appointment may discourage you from canceling your workout in favor of work. My aunt has a walking partner she meets up with early every morning; I used to play tennis with an attorney. Another trick is to integrate your exercise into your work: ride your bike or roller blade to a Federal Express office, or walk to the library to do some research.

The following information will help you develop an exercise program and will provide some basic tips on how to do it right.

Cardiovascular

Thirty minutes of cardiovascular (aerobic) activity at least three times a week can improve your mood and enhance your creative thinking. To burn body fat, you'd need to keep your heart rate up for about an hour. But the big bonus is that cardiovascular training is great for your heart and lungs. And even though medical science has made great strides in transplanting these organs, keeping your own set in good working condition is the preferred method.

To determine whether you are working your heart and lungs at the ideal rate (60 percent of your capacity) for your age, use the following formula: Subtract your age from 226 and your resting heart rate from that. Multiply the result by 60 percent and then add your resting heart rate. For example, if you're forty years old and your resting heart rate is 70:

$$226 - 40 - 70 = 116 \times .60 = 69.6 + 70 = 139.6$$

Take your impulse near the top of your exercise exertion or buy a heart rate monitor at a sporting goods store. Try to keep your rate close to your 60 percent goal without going over it.

If you find that daunting, training experts I spoke with advocate this simple method of creating an exercise program that keeps your heart at the right rate:

- ▶ Start your program (walking, biking, etc.) at a rate that feels comfortable to you. You don't need to get winded or exhausted, but you should be able to break a sweat and feel your heart rate increase.
- ▶ Do the exercise for twenty to thirty minutes.
- ▶ Stay at this level for one week.
- ▶ The following week, work the same amount of time, but increase your distance or speed. Run an extra mile or add some more uphill climbs to your bike ride.

Types of Aerobic Exercise

You don't have to be in training for a marathon to get the right amount of aerobic exercise. There are a wide variety of different workouts you can try, depending on your likes and dislikes, where you live, what type of exercise your prefer, and so forth. Here are just a few to help you choose the ones that are right for you:

Walking

Fast Walking

Jogging

Running

Swimming

Bicycling

Hiking

Dancing/dance classes

Aerobics classes/workout videotapes

Cross-country skiing

Snow-shoeing

Rowing

Karate/martial arts

Boxing

Active team sports (basketball, volleyball)

Although many of these are outdoor activities, their workouts can be mirrored using various machines. For example, a NordicTrack provides the upper- and lower- body workouts that come from cross-country skiing; walking and running can be done on a treadmill.

▶ Stay at this level for one week, or until it feels comfortable, then increase your exertion another notch.

▶ Keep doing the exercise and increasing your level of difficulty each week, moving on to the next level after the old one is no longer taxing to you.

Strength Training

Your body starts losing muscle mass after about age twenty-five. And unless you get moving, you're on a physical downward slide from then on. This can manifest itself in health problems, such as heart disease and osteoporosis when you hit your forties, fifties, and sixties. That's the grim news.

The exciting news is that several recent studies with people in their eighties indicate that strength training can yield dramatic results even at advanced ages. So, even if you have already experienced muscle mass loss, you can benefit from exercise. According to nationally recognized fitness expert Kathy Smith, a well-known study put men and women from eighty-six to ninety years old on an aggressive training program (enough weight so that you can only do twelve reps without muscle fatigue). The results after two months showed a 175 percent increase in strength. Two people from the group of twelve stopped using their canes entirely. You, of course, don't have to wait until you're eighty or ninety to enjoy the impressive results of a good training program.

 Word on Motivation

Kathy Smith, who has created dozens of best-selling and award-winning fitness videos and is the author of several health-and-fitness books, gave me an interesting insight into why many people have a hard time sticking with an exercise regimen, even though they may start out with enthusiasm and the best intentions. Here's what she said:

"Most of us begin with surface reasons, like we're self-conscious about flabby thighs, or wiggly arms. But when you have deadlines, responsibilities, or you're just plain tired, that motivation isn't enough. You'll think of something like 'Oh well, I'll just wear long sleeves this summer or long pants instead of shorts.'

"It's easy to find reasons why you can't exercise and easy to come up with reasons why you don't really have to anyway. Obviously, the surface reasons just don't keep you going. But if you can grasp the 'big picture'—the life enhancement and interpersonal reasons—then you've got something solid that will get you out there even if you've got to work around deadlines and fatigue.

"The big-picture reasons would be something like, 'I feel edgy at the end of the day; I snap at my family; my sex life is declining; I'm too tired to play with my kids on the weekend.' Then it's not just about flabby thighs, it's about your life, self-esteem, energy, stress, tolerance for rejection, obstacles, hassles, and so forth. Plus, you know that if you've just drunk two cups of coffee to get going and your shoulders are tight, you don't handle things as well as when you've just come in from a run and feel relaxed, energetic, and ready to cope!"

Push-ups, abdominal crunches, squats with weights—you can do any of these at home. Using good form will ensure that you get good results from your strength-training efforts. Most important, good form is essential for avoiding injury. If you are new to exercise, I urge you to consult a training professional to get you started doing your weight-bearing exercises correctly.

Stretches

Quick stretches done at your desk can get the blood flowing and loosen up your muscles in a way that will restore your spirits and make you feel wonderful. Here are some basic stretches to try.

Triceps, lats, and lower back:

- ▶ Sitting in your chair, raise one arm straight up.
- ▶ Bend arm at elbow, dropping hand down behind your head with elbow next to ear.
- ▶ Bend sideways at waist toward opposite side. Keep back straight.
- ▶ Breathe and hold until you feel a good stretch.

Arm and upper back

- ▶ Sitting in chair, reach between knees and grab front of chair with both hands.
- ▶ Relax upper back between shoulder blades and lean backward.
- ▶ Keep head level and spine straight.
- ▶ Relax, breathe, hold until you feel good stretch between shoulder blades as they are pulled forward.

Chest, shoulder, and biceps

- ▶ Stand or sit.
- ▶ Put the thumb and index finger side of your fist against a wall or doorframe at shoulder height.
- ▶ Spin your chair or turn your body away from the wall, pulling the arm behind you.
- ▶ Breathe; focus on relaxing anything that feels stretched.

Gluts and hips

- ▶ Sitting, place your right ankle on top of your left knee, as if you were sitting casually.
- ▶ Grasp your foot and knee and pull up to your chest and lean forward into your leg.
- ▶ Hold for the stretch; breathe and relax.

Using Role Models

Kathy Smith maintains that a majority of this country's top CEOs exercise vigorously at least three times a week. These are men and women running multibillion-dollar corporations who make exercise a priority in their busy schedules. Why do they do it?

▶ *Stress reduction.* A good workout allows your body to release tensions.

▶ *Energy and creativity boost* from an early morning workout. Many exercising CEO's say that they frequently have great ideas while working out on the treadmill or Stairmaster.

▶ *Recreation and escape* from the grind. They like doing it and think it's fun!

▶ *Health.* These successful men and women know that they are valuable assets to their companies and want to take care of themselves accordingly. As a result, they have fewer sick days, less downtime from back pain, fatigue, and so forth.

Water—Learn to Love It

You may have heard or read the advice that you should drink at least eight to ten glasses of water a day. This may seem impossible to you, but once you get into the habit of drinking loads of water, you will want to drink this much and maybe more. One way to help yourself increase your intake is to keep a 64-ounce jug of water—the body's minimum daily requirement—on your desk. As you deplete the pitcher, you will see the progress you are making. To encourage yourself to drink more water, consider the following:

▶ The human body is 80 percent water (not cola, coffee, or juice).

▶ Every chemical reaction that occurs in your brain requires water.

▶ By the time you feel thirsty, your body is already dehydrated.

▶ Even a 2 percent reduction in your amount of body water will make you less productive. Problem solving, making judgments, responding quickly—are all affected at this level. A 5 percent reduction can seriously impair mental functioning.

▶ Sometimes when you feel fatigued, what you're really experiencing is dehydration.

▶ Less hydration in the body means that thirsty muscles and joints wear out faster.

In his book *Spontaneous Healing,* Dr. Andrew Weil provides some recommendations for ensuring that the water you drink is free of toxins (including industrial waste runoff, acid rain, agricultural chemicals, and debris from water pipes). If you're concerned about drinking tap water, there are a number of filtration systems on the market. The right system for you will be determined by what you want to filter out of your water. Many systems only take away odors and tastes and do not remove harmful ingredients from water. Filtration systems, in order of the amount of elements they remove from water, include steam distillation (the most effective), reverse osmosis, and carbon filters. You will have to weigh convenience, cost, and health concerns to determine the best method for attaining clean water.

Drinking bottled water is another option as long as you choose the water carefully. The purity of bottled water varies widely from brand to brand. Some basics rules: Do not drink water that has a taste or smell. A taste or smell of plastic in the water you drink can represent a dissolution of plastic into the water. If you choose to drink bottled water, you can order and have delivered a freestanding watercooler for your home office.

> **I**f you don't like the taste of water, try adding a slice of lemon or lime to your glass.

Water Stealers

If you regularly use any of these items, be aware that they dehydrate you. Compensate by increasing the amount of water you drink.

▶ Coffee and tea—for each cup, you need about 2 cups of water

▶ Carbonated, caffeinated sodas

- Decongestants, antihistamines, many prescription drugs
- Dry air (from indoor heat in the winter, from outdoor heat in desert areas)
- Pollution and pollen—they cause your body to "flush" at a faster rate
- Alcohol—the biggest dehydrator of all

Many of the beverages we sip without thinking about them are the stealth weapons of weight gain. You may eat like the proverbial bird, but if you're sipping sodas, fruit juices, or sweetened teas or coffees all day, you are getting a caloric overload that your body will convert to fat.

Sleep

Sleeping odd and irregular hours is an easy habit to get into when you work at home, because you can easily stay up working into the wee hours and then try to catch up by sleeping late or taking naps. And because your business phone can ring at any time of the night or day, you may be tempted to put work first and sleep second. This is a trap because sleeping regular hours is as important to your body as sleeping enough hours. If you habitually rob your sleep to give extra time to your work, your job performance is the very thing that will suffer in the long run.

Unlike water and exercise, sleep is one of the physical requirements your body asks for in very insistent ways. Despite this, most people do not get as much sleep as they need.

According to the National Institutes of Health Sleep Center, the typical American is sleep deprived. A 1997 research study concluded that the average person needs 8.1 hours of sleep each night—but gets only about 6.9. In other words, you're an hour and twenty minutes short right now.

A recent National Sleep Foundation Gallup survey revealed that nearly half of all U.S. adults acknowledge that daytime sleepiness interferes with their routine daily activities. And many sleep experts agree that a majority of adults no longer know what it feels like to be fully alert.

How to Determine If You Are Getting Enough Sleep

It is normal to feel a midafternoon "slump," but feeling very sleepy in the midafternoon isn't normal. Here are some symptoms of too little sleep that you may not have recognized. Make a check mark next to the items that are true for you a fair amount of the time.

____ 1.   You rarely wake up in the morning without the alarm clock.

____ 2.   Upon awakening, you don't look forward to the day ahead.

____ 3.   Getting out of bed is a painful chore.

____ 4.   You drop things, bump into furniture, and are generally more clumsy than you used to be.

____ 5.   Your eyes feel tired and look puffy well into the late morning.

____ 6.   You don't really feel like talking to other people in the morning (and you used to enjoy it).

____ 7.   You feel a little sick until you've been up for a few minutes.

____ 8.   You often nod off in gatherings or at events that you'd prefer to be alert for.

____ 9.   Even the simple tasks seem like more than you can comfortably do.

____ 10.   You frequently fall asleep when reading.

____ 11.   Sex seems to require more energy than you've got.

____ 12.   You are grumpy, brusque, or impatient with people.

____ 13.   You make more mistakes—large and small—than is normal for you.

Count up your check marks. If you checked more than five of these statements as true for you most of the time, you should attempt to increase the amount of sleep you get. You may not need to increase the amount of sleep you get by hours every night, you may only be getting a few minutes too little sleep. See the sections below on sleep schedules and napping to determine how you can make these adjustments.

The U.S. National Highway Traffic Safety Administration estimates that approximately 100,000 police-reported crashes annually (about 1.5 percent of all crashes) involve drowsiness or fatigue as a principal causal factor. A conservative estimate of related fatalities is 1,500 annually, or 4 percent of all traffic crash deaths.

How to figure out how much sleep you need. Now that you know you aren't getting enough sleep, how do you find out just how much you should be getting? Despite the NIH's precise statistic for the average person, the right amount of sleep for you may vary. You will need to do a trial-and-error test. At each stage of this experiment, pay attention to how you feel: Do you wake up without the alarm? Do you feel refreshed or groggy? How do you feel as the day goes on, energetic or sleepy and sluggish? How are you doing by Friday night? Game for a movie and pizza? Or dying to flake out and get to bed early?

Start by sleeping eight hours for five nights. If you feel fine and aren't experiencing any sleep deprivation symptoms, then go no further. You're an eight-hour-a-day person.

If eight hours don't appear to be enough, add fifteen minutes at a time and stay with it for a week. Try to get to bed by the same hour every night and get up at the same time each morning.

Consider your experiment successfully completed when you've gone through a week waking up refreshed and feeling few or none of the symptoms listed above.

Naps

If you resist napping because you think it is lazy, consider this list of famous nappers: Winston Churchill slept for one hour after lunch each day, John D. Rockefeller slept for thirty minutes each day at noon, and Eleanor Roosevelt closed her eyes or napped for twenty minutes before important presentations whenever possible. One of the benefits of working at home is that you can take advantage of this great energy booster.

If you are new to napping, this advice may help you get started. Here's what the experts advise for doing it right.

▶ Pick the right time. Ideally, take your nap between 2 and 4 P.M. These are the times when our diurnal rhythm tends to make us most sleepy. In other cultures, this is called siesta time. Also, if you nap much later in the day, you may interfere with nighttime sleep.

▶ Keep it short. Nap no longer than forty minutes. This will keep you from losing sleep at night and also from getting into such a deep sleep that you wake up groggy.

▶ If you can't bring yourself to grab twenty minutes from the afternoon, you might want to try catnaps. They aren't for everyone, but some people can go off by themselves where no phones will ring and close their eyes for just five minutes or so. They get up feeling remarkably refreshed and rested.

If you're suffering from insomnia, stay away from naps because they'll just make it that much harder to get to sleep at night. And remember that sleeping in a regular pattern is important.

Food

When I speak to groups of home-based workers, I am often asked about how to keep eating under control. The double-edged sword—or should I say knife?—of freedom at home has many of us cutting out of the office and down to the kitchen for snacks.

There's nothing inherently wrong with snacking. But it can be a problem if you're skipping meals and then using snacks to fill yourself up and give you a quick energy boost later in the afternoon. Skipped meals sap your energy and snacks trying to double for real meals tend to be of the fattening variety, such as candy bars, hunks of cheese, salted peanuts by the fistful. You're better off taking the time to fix yourself the kind of lunch that will keep you going for a few hours.

It's not uncommon for people working at home to use food in a variety of ways that aren't particularly productive or good for them. They snack instead of fixing meals, eat to cope with boredom, indulge in large and long lunches in the middle of the day, munch just to be doing something while taking a break. In short, we eat because we can: it's there all day long.

There are also food temptations in a traditional office, but probably fewer than you'll find at home. And when you work around other people, you might be embarrassed to go back for that third donut or piece of birthday cake. At home, there is no one to raise an eyebrow. But if you're not mindful of your eating, working at home could cause you to raise your weight substantially.

The single best thing I can tell you about dealing with food in the home office is *If it's there, you will eat it.*

This isn't a curse; it's a simple statement of fact. Human nature, hunger, schedules—all these conspire to make you grab food that's handy. Put another way, if you wait until you're hungry to find something to eat, you probably won't be eating something healthy. Once you realize this, you're way ahead of the game in controlling your daytime eating. The trick is to make sure that the food within your grabbing range is good for you.

Plan Ahead

The way to make sure that you keep your eating habits healthy is to go the grocery store with the "If it's there . . ." plaque in one hand and a carefully drawn up shopping list in the other. Here are some tips on planning.

▶ Think about your week's lunches and dinners on a Sunday evening, or at least a few days ahead. Plan dinners that can generate leftovers for lunch—a large stir-fry, a chicken-and-vegetable casserole, chili, or soups.

▶ Wash and cut up vegetables and keep them on hand for snacking. Most grocery stores also sell prewashed and cut vegetables.

▶ Avoid buying temptation foods such as ice cream, chips, candy bars, cookies, and the like. Foods you can substitute for high-fat snacks include prewashed baby carrots, celery sticks, rice cakes, dried fruit, low-fat yogurt, flavored seltzer, herbal tea, baked tortilla chips, humus, pretzels, and flat bread. A word of caution about foods in the grocery store labeled as low-fat: If you eat enough of them, you can still put on weight. Read labels carefully, and don't assume that you can eat endless amounts of them without accruing calories.

How Smart Do You Eat?

I am not an expert in nutrition or medicine, so I recommend conducting some research of your own into the health benefits of a modified diet. I base my advice here on my own experiences with dietary changes and the positive increases in energy and health as a result of them.

My personal recommendations for diet are to eat lots of organic vegetables, whole grains, and low-fat protein. This diet is rich in antioxidants, which help keep your immune system strong, and provides you with the vitamins and minerals you need and the fiber your system requires. Steering clear of processed foods and the chemical preservatives they contain is another good goal. I also believe that it is a good idea to keep sugar, caffeine, and other substances that artificially stimulate your system to a minimum.

This isn't to say that you can't eat the occasional hamburger or hot fudge sundae; I certainly do. Recommendations for dietary restrictions are something to strive for and work toward gradually. If you would like to improve your diet and thereby your energy level, I suggest that you visit a nutritionist. A qualified professional can help you determine what allergies you have and what kind of dietary changes you can institute to suit your body and your lifestyle.

Creating an Injury-Free Work Space 12

Creating a safe and efficient work environment is a challenge for every home-based worker. While you have the advantage of creating an office that is as comfortable as you choose to make it, you also have no one around to guide you through the process. Because so many home offices are driven by computer technology, you are at risk of suffering injuries such as carpal tunnel syndrome and other repetitive stress disorders. Neck, shoulder, wrist, or back pain may seem minor at first, but all can be debilitating and have a serious impact on your ability to perform your job. In this chapter, I show you why you need to be concerned about computer injuries, and what you can do to prevent them. You'll learn the right way to sit and type, and you'll find out what to look for in critical pieces of office equipment.

The Realities of
Computer Injuries

If you think that you're not likely to get a workplace injury, think again. Chances are, as a home-based worker, you spend more time at your computer than other workers. And if that's the case, you're more prone to computer-related disorders, such as repetitive stress injury (RSI) and cumulative trauma disorder (CTD), the fastest-growing workplace injuries, according to the National Institute for Occupational Safety and Health. In fact, according to the Occupational Safety and Health Administration (OSHA), RSIs are the largest category of workers' compensation claims.

Also, unlike your corporate counterparts, you don't have immediate access to a human resources or worker safety department to tell you what to do. So you're probably on your own to devise an office layout that works for you, figure out the right way to sit and work, and purchase the right kind of equipment.

I know all this from personal experience. Several years ago, I began feeling a pain in my wrist and shoulder from all the work I was doing on my computer. It got so bad at one point that even holding a toothbrush was hard. I was forced to take severe action. I went on a strict exercise program to strengthen my upper back; I began doing stretches for my hands and wrists; and I had to change the way I worked by creating a system that fit my body type and work habits. I now have both a keyboard that minimizes stress on my wrists, and a good chair, and I follow as many of the rules of avoiding workplace injury as are necessary to keep myself pain-free.

One of the problems with creating an efficient, safe, ergonomic workplace is that there are few tried-and-true rules. Many injuries are a result of interrelated factors. For example, poor body position, which can bring about many different types of RSIs, may be the result of any number of things—the design of your chair, the height of your desk, the placement of your keyboard or monitor, or even your lighting.

And even if you can design your environment to remove all undue stress, you still may injure yourself through overwork. Long hours spent at your computer or your desk can result in strain to your muscles, tendons, and other body parts. That's why many workplace safety experts maintain that there is no substitute to taking frequent breaks and limiting your work time.

Types of Common Injuries

Repetitive Stress Injuries

Repetitive stress injuries, or RSIs, are related to repeated motions such as typing or manipulating a mouse. Poor posture, badly designed equipment, and overuse all contribute to your risk of developing these. The precise cause of many RSIs is unclear, but it is believed that repeated small motions injure tissue in your fingers, hands, wrists, or arms. Although you may not immediately feel these minor traumas, over time they begin to take their toll and cause inflammation and pain.

These disorders are hardly new. In 1893 *Gray's Anatomy* described "peritendinitis crepitans" as occurring in washerwomen, and this affliction was so common that it became known as "washerwoman's thumb." Telegraph operators at the turn of the century suffered from similar disorders caused by their work activities. It took the personal computer explosion of the 1980s to bring these injuries to the forefront, and since 1987 they have been the number one occupational disorder.

You've probably heard of one of the most common RSIs—carpal tunnel syndrome. In this injury, repeated use causes tendons in your wrists to swell, putting pressure on the median nerve as it passes through the narrow passage called the carpal tunnel. Pressure on the nerve causes pain, numbness and other symptoms in the hand. But because the fibers that make up the median nerve actually originate in your neck, anything that affects the nerve anywhere along its course—including the neck and upper chest—can cause these symptoms and make them worse.

When I had problems with my wrist, I discovered that they were the result of a weak upper back. Because my upper back was not strong enough to take the strain of the amount of typing I do, my wrists and forearms were strained. I built up my upper back using very light weights and exercises prescribed by a physical therapist. In addition, I had to wear a special wrist guard when I typed to keep me from bending my injured wrist. I also had to wear the brace at night, because many people reinjure their wrists by curling their wrists when they sleep.

Visual Problems and Headaches

The visual aspect of computer use causes another key workplace-related injury—vision problems. Your eyes were not designed to cope with the close focusing that computers demand. Staring at a computer monitor without a break eventually takes its toll in the form of eyestrain. In addition, when you work with a bright light source such as a computer monitor, television, or movie screen, you tend to blink less. This causes symptoms such headaches or itching, burning eyes. You might also find that your vision deteriorates faster than you expect.

Interestingly, some workplace injury experts believe that vision problems may be more prevalent than RSIs. It's just that many people consider them an inescapable side effect of using a computer. As a result, they fail to report them.

Although eye strain is a common cause of headaches, there may be other reasons too. Poor head and neck posture is one possible cause. Stress is another.

Wrist Resting Syndrome

There has been a lot of discussion recently about "wrist resting syndrome," which has symptoms similar to those of carpal tunnel, but which demands a different treatment.

Most computer users rest their wrists on the table. This concentrates the weight of the arms and hands directly on a highly vulnerable two square inches at the wrist over the unprotected median nerve. With wrist resting syndrome, the damage comes from the force of external contact pressure, not from swelling in the carpal tunnel. Splinting or the use of a rigid wrist brace, common treatments for RSIs, only adds to the pressure. Instead, relief can be sought through a padded glove that diverts pressure from the median nerve.

What to Do If You Suffer from These Illnesses

If you are suffering any kind of pain from working on a computer, consult a physician immediately. These symptoms rarely get better and frequently get much worse. It is never a good idea to try to work through an injury by ignoring it. Try to keep yourself aware of any pain you feel in your fingers, hands, wrists, arms, shoulders, or back. You might even want to keep a short log of any unusual symptoms you experience, and provide this information to your physician or therapist should you need treatment.

Be aware that although most physicians have heard of carpal tunnel and other RSIs, not all are familiar with or properly trained in the treatment of these injuries. Your best bet may be to look for a board-certified physician who specializes in hand surgery, orthopedics, or physical or occupational medicine. Your primary care physician should be able to recommend this type of specialist to you, or you can ask other computer users you know for a reference. Don't be afraid to interview a doctor before you go for treatment—ask if he or she has experience diagnosing this type of injury and what kind of treatment they usually recommend (this will give you an idea to their approach to therapy). And if you don't like the advice you're getting, you can always ask for another opinion. There's no need to go through therapy or even surgery if you don't have to.

There are other types of practitioners who treat RSIs—chiropractors, physical therapists, and hand therapists, to name a few. You might also seek relief from alternative medicine sources such as acupuncture, acupressure, massage, or meditation.

Of course, if you're suffering from vision problems or headaches, you should consult with an ophthalmologist or optometrist.

Preventing Injury before It Happens

Prevention is the key to avoiding workplace injuries. It's imperative for you to take certain precautions—sitting properly, trying low-stress typing, positioning your equipment correctly, and taking frequent breaks.

Take the time to turn these suggestions into habits. They may not seem comfortable at first, but you'll find yourself suffering less strain and trauma as they become second nature.

How to Sit

Proper posture is key to preventing many kinds of muscle or tendon strains. In fact, sitting incorrectly can put so much stress on your body that you start to feel pains in places that you didn't even think you were using—for example, you might hurt your shoulder because your feet aren't placed properly.

To start, you do not need to sit straight up. The angle between your seat and the back of your chair can range anywhere from 85 degrees (slightly forward) to 120 degrees (reclining)—whatever is most comfortable for you. It is actually okay to work while reclining. In fact, it takes strain off your back and wrists.

Your arms should be at your sides, not stretching forward or sticking behind you. Your elbows should be bent at a 90-degree angle, and when your hands are touching your keyboard, they should be at the same height as your elbows. If you're using armrests, they should support your forearms but not be so high as to make you hunch your shoulders.

The seat of your chair should be low enough for your feet to rest firmly on the floor. It should also be high enough so that your thighs are parallel to the floor. If you let your feet dangle, you'll put pressure on your thighs and restrict circulation to your legs. If necessary, you might even want to consider raising your feet by using a phone book or a footrest.

How to Type

As mentioned earlier, your arms are at your sides, elbows bent 90 degrees, with your hands at the same height as your elbows. If your keyboard can't be positioned at this height, you should consider getting an extender tray whose height can be adjusted. The extender tray will also bring the keyboard closer to your body. You need to maintain what's known as wrist-neutral position, which means your wrists lie flat when you type.

Ideally, your wrists should be raised slightly above the keyboard so that your fingers, not your arms, can do all the work. But this isn't a perfect world, and most people I know are more comfortable resting their wrists or palms in front of the keyboard. If that's the case, buy one of those foam rubber wrist rests that attaches to the front of the keyboard. Just be sure to rest your palms, *not your wrists*, on it.

Don't pound on the keys—this can put stress on your fingers as well as on your elbows and shoulders. Instead, type lightly, using just enough force to depress the keys.

Your mouse should be positioned next to your keyboard, preferably on the same tray (be sure to buy one large enough to fit both your keyboard and your pointing device). Reaching up or to the side for your mouse will cause strain on your wrist and shoulder. If you use a numeric keypad, you might want to consider using your mouse with your left hand.

Be sure to hold your mouse correctly. Don't grip it tightly. You should rest your hand on it and move it gently. If you're not doing highly precise work such as graphics, you might want to adjust the mouse tracking (the speed by which the mouse moves the cursor). A higher speed will allow the cursor to move a greater distance with less effort from the mouse.

Setting Up Your Desk, Computer, and Office

The placement of your equipment is critical to maintaining an effective work environment.

As I mentioned before, your keyboard should be directly in front of you, with your mouse or other pointing device next to it. You will cause undue arm strain if you have to reach to the side to type or have to crank your wrist to get to your mouse.

Similarly, you should also put your monitor directly in front of you, at least 16 inches from your eyes. I've seen many furniture ads in which the monitor is off to the side, but if you have to turn your head to look at it, you will put a lot of stress on your neck and shoulders. The top of your monitor should be at eye level. If it's higher than that, you may end up tilting your head back to read it, and this causes headaches.

Try to keep any items you use constantly (phone, pens, pads, Rolodex) within 15 to 20 inches of you. Try not to put any frequently used equipment in an out-of-the-way place where you have to awkwardly reach for it. For example, if you frequently send and receive faxes, put your fax machine in a place that you can reach by swiveling your chair. If you have to reach or stretch, chances are that you will wrench your back or shoulders.

Take Frequent Breaks

This is one suggestion I can't stress enough. When you're in the throes of an exciting project, it may be hard to tear yourself away from your computer. But your body requires rest and breaks. Get up from your desk and move your head, neck, shoulders, arms, and legs. Stand up and walk around while you're on the phone. Try some basic stretches to work out the kinks. Close your eyes for a minute to relieve itching and other strain.

Learn from Concert Pianists

If you spend a lot of time at your computer keyboard in your profession, you can probably learn a lot from other professionals who spend a lot of time at keyboards—concert pianists. Take a look at these observations of how concert pianists sit and play, and see how you can relate it to how you work:

- They sit upright, but relaxed, without back support, on a bench that they adjust to their own height and the height of their piano.

- They take a brief time before playing to adjust their position and get comfortable at their keyboard.

- They use their fingers, not their whole hand, to press the keys, and they don't rest their wrists, but keep them in a neutral position.

- They move their trunk, head, hips, and limbs in a coordinated manner to allow free movement of their hands, wrists, and arms.

- They take short breaks between movements; at intermission, they get up and walk around.

Buy the Right Equipment

As any number of workplace-injury attorneys will tell you, the best work habits won't compensate for poorly designed equipment. Although there have been many advancements in office equipment, much of it is still not designed with the user's comfort and health in mind.

The key is to find equipment that fits your shape and your work habits. Someone who is 5' 2" probably won't be comfortable at a desk designed for someone who is 6' 4". Hands come in different shapes and sizes, too, so a keyboard that's right for one person might cause stress for another. If you're a graphic designer, you might need a different mouse from someone who just uses a computer for word processing needs. It's important to try things out so that you can find what's most comfortable for you and the way you work.

Your Chair

You probably spend more time in your office chair than you do anywhere else, except maybe your bed. Unfortunately, this is an item on which many home office workers seem to penny-pinch, and they pay the price in the form of a sore back, sore shoulders, sore legs, and other body strain.

When I look at design magazines that feature home office layouts, I'm often aghast at what they think constitutes a good office chair. I've seen everything from a fully embroidered Queen Anne to a wicker chair on casters, to one of those metal folding chairs you squirm in at your local PTA meeting. These may work in the style of the room, but none pass the test in the four main chair categories—support, comfort, adjustability, and flexibility.

Support. Your chair should support both your lower and your middle back. For your lower back, put your hand on the small of your back and see if it's permanently bolstered by the backrest. Although lumbar cushions are available to add extra support to this area, you shouldn't need them if your chair is right. When you sit in your chair, you should also feel support in your middle back—the area just below your shoulder blades. Last, if you use armrests, they should be adjustable so that they can be high enough to support your forearms but not so high as to raise your shoulders.

Comfort. Just because a seat offers you good support doesn't mean that it has to be uncomfortable. In fact, you want just the opposite, because sitting in an uncomfortable chair will cause you to squirm and put your body in positions that can cause stress and strain. Make sure that the chair is adequately padded with foam that is both dense enough to support your weight evenly and resilient enough to maintain its shape, comfort, and support over time.

Adjustability. Look for a chair that changes to fit your body, because you never want to have to change your posture to fit the chair. It's best to have multiple adjustment points for back and lumbar support height, back angle, seat height, tilt angle and lock, tilt tension, arm height and width, and swivel. The more points of adjustment, the better, so keep an eye out for models that allow you to make these adjustments independently. And make sure that you can reach all the adjustment controls while you're seated.

Backless Chairs

In your search for the perfect desk chair, you may come across backless chairs, in which you sit in a kind of a squat, with your knees resting and supporting you on a front bar or pad. These are supposed to help prevent lower back pain by shifting some of your weight from your lower back to your knees.

At best, this type of chair is an interesting gadget that might help you for an hour or so a day. And although I know some people who swear by them, backless chairs fail in terms of adjustability and flexibility, and many doubt the veracity of their "support" claims.

> **N**ever buy a chair without trying it out first. Everyone's
> body is different, and fits different chairs differently. If you
> buy your chair by mail order, make sure you can return it for
> a full refund.

Flexibility. It would be nice to think that you can sit in perfect posture all the time. But over the course of the day, you will likely move around a lot—sitting up straight in the morning, slumping during the afternoon, reclining while speaking on the phone, leaning forward to write some notes, and so on. Get a chair that lets you fidget by swiveling, rocking, and tilting.

Your Desk

Whether you go for a big executive model or you're content with a piece of laminated plywood over two filing cabinets, you need to take certain precautions with your desk.

The first thing to look at is size. How much room do you need? Remember, you need room to fit your computer, your monitor, your keyboard, your printer, any other computer peripherals, your phone, your "active files," and anything else you use every day. You will also need enough room to write properly—you don't want to have to move your computer keyboard or scrunch your legs every time you have to jot notes on a pad. Many people prefer an L-shaped desk, with the computer on one stem, and the writing area on the other, so that they can shift between tasks by swiveling their chair.

Next, judge the height of the desk. There should be at least 2 inches of clearance between the top of your thighs and the bottom of the desk or keyboard tray. Typical computer desks, by the way, are 27 inches high; the average writing desk is 30 inches high.

Look for a pull-out keyboard tray. Make sure the tray has enough room not only for the keyboard but for your pointing device as well, so that you don't have to stretch to use your mouse or trackball. Also look for a tray that you can adjust in terms of height—these are often called articulated trays. By the way, if your desk does not come with a keyboard tray, many ergonomic-products distributors sell them as add-ons.

Computer Keyboard

Keyboards have been singled out as the main contributor to various RSIs, especially those that affect the wrists, hands, and fingers. Computer makers have been known to scrimp on the keyboard, so you should consider upgrading the one that came with your system. Here's what to look for:

▶ The keys should provide a comfortable level of resistance—more than a minimal amount of force to activate, but not so much that they're hard to press.

▶ There should be some kind of feedback (either sound or touch) so that you can tell that you've pressed the key hard enough to activate it.

▶ Make sure that your keyboard has an adjustable tilt mechanism so that it can lie flat or be angled to fit your typing style.

Keyboard Gimmicks. Because there is no such thing as an "ergonomic seal of approval," you're likely to run into many products that purport to offer ergonomic benefits when there may actually be no hard

Food for Thought

You might think that the word *ergonomic* connotes ease of use and efficiency, but product marketers have begun to overuse the term. In fact, I recently saw a reference to a tortilla chip that touted its "unique ergonomic shape" with "an easy thumb and forefinger grip" for easy dipping. The lesson: Don't assume that something will be comfortable simply because it is labeled ergonomic.

data to support these claims. One such product is a "split" keyboard, which, as the name suggests, is split down the middle and has the keys at an angle to reduce wrist and arm strain by keeping them in a neutral position. Some people love these devices, but some ergonomics experts say that split keyboards don't really do much to improve wrist position. These new keyboards have, for the most part, failed to catch on because it's very hard to change the way you type.

There are some gimmicks that do work, however. A keyboard with a built-in trackball may be a good idea if you use this pointing device, because it will limit your arm and hand movement. If you're left-handed, you might want to look for a keyboard with a detachable numeric keypad, so you can put it on the left side.

Pointing Device

Your mouse may be just as dangerous as your keyboard in terms of repetitive stress injuries. It may not fit your hand, or you may not be using it correctly. And again, like a keyboard, this is a common area where computer companies try to get away with offering something cheap, so you may want to replace the one that came with your system.

When shopping for a mouse, choose one that fits comfortably in your cupped hand. Pay attention to where the keys are located and to how they feel. Are they easy to reach? Do they provide the right amount of resistance? Also check the weight of the mouse—does it feel substantial in your hand or does it feel too light or too heavy?

But a mouse isn't the only pointing device you can use. Many people who experience wrist, hand, or shoulder pain have switched to a trackball, which is stationary, thus requiring less arm and hand movement. Pay close attention to the resistance of your trackball—if it is too easy or too hard to manipulate, you may be putting too much stress on the small muscles in your hand and fingers. Touchpads (where you use your finger to adjust the cursor by moving along a small pad attached to the keyboard) are another alternative, but many people find it hard to move the cursor accurately with this type of system. If you do a lot of graphics work, you might want to consider using a pen-based input system such as a drawing tablet.

Monitor

Computer monitors are a chief source of eyestrain and other vision problems—flicker, resolution, sharpness, and even screen size can have an impact. To be kind to your eyes, find a screen with a resolution of at least 640 × 480, although 1024 × 768 is even better. The sharpness of the image is measured in "dot pitch"—the lower the number, the sharper the image. You want the dot pitch to measure .31 or less. Don't get anything smaller than a 15-inch screen, and with prices coming down, you should consider getting a 17-inch or larger monitor.

In addition, make sure that you can adjust the height of your monitor. It also should swivel, so you can get rid of any annoying reflections and glare. Most monitors come with some kind of antiglare coating. Separate antiglare screens, which fit over the front of the monitor and reduce glare from windows and lights, can be useful, although some people find that they darken the screen too much.

Phone

Nothing can give you a pain in the neck or shoulder like your phone. Cradling the receiver between your shoulder and ear puts an incredible amount of stress on your neck muscles.

A laptop or other portable computer is an enormous convenience if you're frequently on the road. The problem is that many people use their laptop as their primary computer. This can cause problems, because laptop keyboards and screens are not nearly as sophisticated or as flexible as those available for desktop machines, and it's much harder to place them in the right spot on your desk.

If your laptop is your primary machine, I highly recommend that you get a docking station or port replicator. By plugging your laptop into one of these units, you can use a full-size keyboard and a desktop monitor. Your wrists and eyes will thank you.

When you're shopping for ergonomic products, remember that you may be used to working with "bad" design, and that well-designed products may initially feel, at the very least, awkward. Be sure to test any piece of equipment before you buy it—ask the sales person to take it out of the box and let you try it on or connect it to a computer. Also look for a liberal return policy that lets you bring back anything you don't like after using it for a week or two.

If you're on the phone a lot, consider buying a lightweight headset so you can keep your hands free. These have become increasingly popular home office options, and are available through most telephone stores and catalogs. If you like to roam while you speak, look for a cordless version, preferably one that operates at 900 MHz, which has a long range.

Light and Air

The last things you need to control are the light and air in your work environment. Many external factors—from too much glare to too much noise—can contribute to workplace injuries. Following these guidelines should help you limit your risk.

Light

The cheapest and least tiring form of light is daylight. Natural light will make you more productive, and it is the least stressful on your eyes. Indirect light from north-facing windows is actually best because it is the softest (that's why many painting studios face north). Direct southern light pouring through your window can be problematic—it creates glare and will raise the temperature of your work space. If you face south, invest in a good set of curtains or shades.

For your artificial light, you should look for a balance between ambient and task lighting. Ambient lighting is what lights your room; ideally, it should be bright and indirect (reflected off walls, ceilings, or other surfaces). As a rule, your computer monitor should be as bright as your room's ambient lighting. Task lighting is what you shine directly on to your work. Your task light (preferably in the form of a good, adjustable desk lamp), should be placed directly above what you're working on to avoid shadows.

Be careful not to shine lights into your computer screen. The glare and bright spots will cause eyestrain and headaches. Also, place your monitor at a 90-degree angle to any nearby window. If the window is behind you, you'll end up with glare in your screen. If the window is in front of you, you may find that there's too much contrast between the sun and your screen, also hurting your eyes.

Benefits of Artificial Light

Some people find that sunlight actually affects their demeanor, and that a lack of sunlight saps them of energy and makes them depressed. Think of the winter doldrums that hit some people every November through February, when the days are shortest. They get depressed, put on weight, crave starchy or sugary foods, and require more sleep than usual. At its most extreme clinical level, this is called seasonal affective disorder, or SAD.

If you're one of these people, you might want to consider an artificial light box. A number of studies have recently been taking place at research facilities such as the Winter Depression Program at Columbia-Presbyterian Medical Center that show the benefits of light therapy. The light box consists of a set of fluorescent bulbs installed in a box with a diffusing screen, and it is set up on a table or desktop. The box produces a bright light (2,500–10,000 lux) similar in color composition to outdoor daylight. Different people have different responses, but many have reported highly positive results.

Air

Always work in a comfortable environment. Many people prefer a working temperature of 68°F, and some people work better in warmer or cooler conditions. A simple tweak of the thermostat or a crack of a window can solve many of these problems.

Very low humidity also bothers many people and can cause symptoms such as dry eyes, nose, and mouth. Contact lens wearers are particularly susceptible, because their eyes are usually already dry from blinking less. If you find that your office is too dry, installing a humidifier may help.

RESOURCES

Part I. Emotional Survival

Books

Depression and Its Treatment by John H. Greist, M.D., and James W. Jefferson, M.D. (Warner Books, 1992)

This easily accessible guide explains depression and its causes. It also discusses the various types of treatments, from drugs to psychotherapy.

Endurance: Shackelton's Incredible Voyage by Alfred Lansing (Carroll & Graf, 1986)

A tale of survival on a ship near the South Pole in cold and harsh conditions is so astounding that it would be dismissed as implausible if it were fiction. Any person who feels challenged by the obstacles of running a home office will find this book a good diversion and a source of perspective.

How to Win Friends and Influence People by Dale Carnegie (Pocket Books, reissued 1994)

This essential tool for any businessperson tells you how to engender people with enthusiasm for your ideas and make people like you. With these skills, it is hard not to be successful.

Forbes Greatest Business Stories of All Time by Daniel Gross and the editors of *Forbes* magazine (John Wiley & Sons, 1996)

One of the best ways to motivate yourself is to learn from how other people have succeeded. People profiled in this book include Walt Disney, J. P. Morgan, Henry Ford, Mary Kay Ash, and Sam Walton.

What to Say When You Talk to Yourself by Shad Helmstetter, Ph.D. (Pocket Books, 1990)
> The guru of positive self-talk teaches you how to send yourself positive messages all day, every day, while weeding out the bad ones you're not even aware of yet!

Career Power, 12 Winning Habits to Get You from Where You Are to Where You Want to Be by Richard Koonce (Amacom, 1994)
> How to make the most of your strengths, while coping with changes in your work environment.

Rotten Rejections edited by Andre Bernard (Pushcart Press, 1990)
> Think you're the only one to ever get rejected? Take a look at these literary rejection letters through the ages.

Diamond in the Rough by Barry J. Farber (Berkley, 1995)
> This book, by a leading sales guru, focuses on how to find your own potential. It includes interviews with accomplished entrepreneurs, athletes, politicians, and other successful people in various fields.

Newsletters

These two newsletters are targeted at home office workers and often include motivational articles to help get you through tough times.

The Accidental Entrepreneur
Dixie Darr, editor and publisher
3421 Alcott Street
Denver, CO 80211
Subscriptions are $24 per year for 6 issues

Winning Ways
Barbara Winter, editor and publisher
P.O. Box 39412
Minneapolis, MN 55439
Subscriptions are $31 per year for 6 issues

For Internet Newsgroup and Mailing List Information

Use newsgroups and mailing lists to interact and network with like-minded individuals via the Internet.

▶ DejaNews (http://www.dejanews.com)—the leading directory for finding Usenet newsgroups

▶ Liszt.com (http://www.liszt.com)—directory of mailing lists, along with information on how to subscribe.

Part II. Managing Time and Workload

Burnout: The High Cost of High Achievement by Dr. Herbert Freudenberger (Bantam, 1989)
    The standard text about burnout.

Procrastination: Why You Do It, What to Do About It by Jane B. Burka, Ph.D. and Lenora M. Yuen, Ph.D. (Addison-Wesley, reissued 1990)
    The causes of procrastination, and what you can do to shake them.

Organizing Your Home Office for Success by Lisa Kanarek (Plume, 1993)
    Full of helpful tips, hints, and methods for creating an efficient workplace in your home.

60 Ways to Relieve Stress in 60 Seconds by Manning Rubin (Workman, 1993)
    One of the multitude of stress management guides you'll find at your bookstore. This one has a number of short stress-relief techniques that take less than a minute.

301 Ways to Have Fun at Work by Dave Hemsath and Leslie Yerkes (Berrett-Keohler, 1997)
    As the title describes, this book is full of ways—both outrageous and practical—to make your work fun.

The One Minute Manager by Kenneth Blanchard (Berkley, revised 1993)
    The classic tome for contemporary managers — including self-managers.

Visionary Business by Marc Allen (New World Library, 1995)
A book about mental focus. It is designed to help you set goals and keep your sights on your dream.

Pamphlets

How to File: A Comprehensive Guide for the Office Professional
Esselte Pendaflex, maker of filing systems, offers this free 35-page reference guide with tips and techniques to help you set up an efficient filing system. Call 800-645-6051.

Software

Uninstaller
Luckman International
800-711-2676
If you're running a Windows computer, use Uninstaller to help you perform the tricky, but essential task of reclaiming old disk space. It will remove unused programs from your files and serve up other extraneous files and data so you can remove them at your discretion.

Part III. Integrating Your Work and Private Life

Books

Honey I Want to Start My Own Business: A Planning Guide for Couples by Azriela L. Jaffe (HarperBusiness, 1996)
How to start your own successful business while maintaining a stable family life. Features the real-life experiences of 130 entrepreneurial couples.

Having It All, Having Enough by Deborah Lee, Ph.D. (Amacom, 1997)
Practical ways to strike a successful balance between work and family.

Mompreneurs by Ellen Parlapiano and Patricia Cobe (Perigee, 1996)
A guide for work-at-home moms, this book includes many helpful tips on separating your work time from your mom time.

Groups and Associations

Entrepreneurial Couples Support Network
P.O. Box 209
Bausman, PA 17504
717-872-1890
  National organization to help couples build successful businesses and
  marriages.

MATCH (Mother's Access to Careers at Home)
P.O. Box 123,
Annandale, VA 22003
703-764-2320
  A networking and advocacy group for women who wish to balance their
  families and careers by working from home.

Families and Work Institute
330 Seventh Avenue, 14th floor
New York, NY 10001
212-465-2044
  Provides support and information for working parents.

Part IV. Health

Books

*Kathy Smith's Fitness Makeover: A 10-Week Guide to Exercise and Nutrition
That Will Change Your Life* by Kathy Smith (Warner Books, 1997)
  This workbook includes plans to help you create a sensible eating and
  exercise plan.

Spontaneous Healing by Andrew Weil (Fawcett Columbine, 1995)
  A book by an M.D. who also practices alternative medicine. This book
  provides information on how to create a healthier lifestyle for yourself so
  that your body can keep itself healthy.

Pamphlets

National Sleep Foundation
729 15th St., N.W.
Washington, DC 20005

> The National Sleep Foundation has a wide variety of publications on sleep and various sleep disorders. Tell them what you're interested in (e.g., snoring, sleep apnea) and they'll send you the appropriate pamphlets. Include a SASE with 55 cents postage.

Food Guide Pyramid
U.S. Government Pamphlet Hotline
202-606-8000

> The federal government publishes a free handy guide to the food pyramid, which highlights the various aspects of a balanced diet. You can also order their *U.S. Dietary Guidelines for Americans,* which includes height and weight charts in addition to information about eating.

Center for Office Technology
1800 N. Kent Street, Suite 1160
Rosslyn, VA 22209
703-276-1174

> *Practical Recommendations for the Road Warrior* is a pamphlet written by Bryce Rutter, an ergonomics specialist with the Metaphase Design Group in St. Louis. It contains sensible advice and tips. Price: $5.

Internet

Mayo Health Oasis
http://www.mayo.ivi.com

> Includes news and resources about health and nutrition issues. Brought to you by the Mayo Clinic.

Wellness Interactive Network
http://www.stayhealthy.com

> This directory has lists of World Wide Web–based resources for health, nutrition, and fitness issues.

CUErgo—Cornell Ergonomics Web
http://ergo.human.cornell.edu
> Site of Cornell University's Human Factors and Ergonomics Program. It focuses on ways to improve comfort, performance, and health through the ergonomic design of products and environments.

Ergonomic Products

The following companies and catalogs produce ergonomic products.
Hello Direct
800-520-3311
> For telephone headsets and other phone/telecom products.

AliMed Ergonomics Catalog
800-225-2610
> Includes ergonomic office products.

Ergosource
800-969-4374
> Offers a variety of ergonomic products, including foot rests, keyboards, telephone headsets, monitor supports, etc.

Medtech Surgical
800-769-9515
> Sells antiglare screens, wrist rests, extender trays, mouse extender trays, and other similar products.

INDEX

About the Author

Alice Bredin has helped millions of people around the world learn to thrive in the home office. She writes the popular syndicated newspaper column "Working at Home," and is the author of *The Virtual Office Survival Handbook* (also published by Wiley). Ms. Bredin is the host and resident expert of the American Express Small Business Exchange web site and is featured biweekly on the Hewlett-Packard small business web site. Her New York City–based business, Bredin Business Information, helps Fortune 500 companies market to the home-based and small business market.